FOUR FLATS
AND A PITCH PIPE

My Adventures with the Four Flats Quartet

By

Dick Cadd

With Comments by Helen Cadd...or
"I Married a Quartet"

D1637275

ISBN: 1-4107-9252-8 (e-book)
ISBN: 1-4107-9253-6 (Paperback)

This book is printed on acid free paper.

1stBooks – rev. 11/18/03

TABLE OF CONTENTS

DEDICATION

Roy P. Clark

There is only one man that deserves the honor of this kind of recognition. Roy Clark not only has always been our mentor, but the mentor of an untold number of students during his many years of tutoring.

Roy was such an incredible man that it is difficult for anyone who did not know him to realize that there once was such a valiant figure. We, in the quartet, first met Roy when we entered Pacific College. He was the choral director of a very excellent choir, which traveled the West Coast year after year. Of course, we became much closer when he entered our lives as a quartet member, then later, as a mentor and grand cheerleader.

Roy's contributions did not end with Pacific College, but he went on to encourage many as he became professor at Barclay College in Haviland, Kansas, where he influenced hundreds more of his students.

To this great and humble man whose life was always encouraging others and without whose constant encouragement there would never have been a FOUR FLATS QUARTET, I dedicate this book.

FORWARD

There are a number of people who could write this book better than I, so that in itself was reason enough for me to hesitate. In fact, there were a number of people who **said** they were going to write it and that left it completely out of my thoughts until after more than 50 years had passed. Then, I knew it was now or never; someone had to try to tell the story of an amazing foursome and their unusual adventures.

There were the wives of the quartet who always wanted to write a book titled, I Married a Quartet. Cute. The problem was, it is very difficult to write a book by committee from different parts of the world. Each one was supposed to write a part of it. It didn't happen. Maybe, some day. To be fair, I must give due credit to my wife, Helen, since she did write her own book titled Never To Forget, the story of our family on the mission field. But that was the end of her writing.

Any one of the other three quartet guys is a better writer; I concede that. They each are more meticulous, and certainly more accurate and detailed. I assume that's a virtue when it comes to writing. At least, they have each had more experience in writing than I have.

However, the one thing I have going for me is that I like to "take the bull by the horns" and just do it. This could be my biggest mistake. Nevertheless, I've done it, and that's more than you can say for the many threats and promises over the last fifty years.

In writing such a book I have discovered there is more to leave out than there is to include. It is not possible to cover all the events and experiences of more than fifteen years of travel throughout the world. Nor is it possible to adequately describe the personalities and shenanigans of the three persons I lived with for fifteen years. I have endeavored to lift some of the highlights of these years and I trust I have done it fairly and honestly, if not perfectly.

One thing I discovered early on; each event is seen differently by each individual. Therefore, there could be four books written on this same subject by four different people and you would get four different stories. It is somewhat like the four blind men each trying to describe an elephant. Since each one was feeling a different part (one the tail, one the trunk, one the leg and so forth) of the animal, they all described it differently. So it is in writing this book. This is but one view of the adventures of four.   Perhaps, one day you will see another. Each person had different experiences in background and each had different experiences following our time together.

So, here is my version of 15 years of hilarious, inspirational, ridiculous, challenging, motivational, educational, awesome and wonderful times.

Helen's Comments…

If there is anything that challenges me, it's for someone to tell me I can't do it—or it won't happen. So here's my answer to Dick's statement that one book was the end of my writing.

My husband is right when he says he "takes the bull by the horns and just does it!" Dick has never been known for his patience. So he asked GOD to give him patience, and the LORD gave him me. Doesn't James 1:2-3 say, "Is your life full of difficulty and temptations? Then be happy, for when the way is rough, your patience has a chance to grow. So let it grow, and don't try to squirm out of your problems"

I've given Dick plenty of chance to grow into patience, and he has learned how to put up with my faulty time clock. It seems like I am always late, no matter how hard I try. So Dick takes a Newsweek every place we go.

Dick accomplishes more than anyone I've ever met. He has a "to do" list, and his list almost always gets finished. I doubt if I have ever accomplished my list on time.

Yes, everyone does see things differently—especially if one is a man and the other one is a woman. This is especially true when one travels the world and the other one stays home with children! So here's my version of "I Married a Quartet."

ACKNOWLEDGEMENTS

It is always dangerous to start naming people who have helped in a project for fear of unintentionally leaving someone out. But I will make the effort nonetheless.

Without a doubt, there would be no book with my name on it if it were not for my grandson Jesse Cadd. His expertise with the computer, arranging photos, and generally putting together this script left both Helen and me in amazement. I am eternally indebted and grateful for his knowledge, patience, and expertise.

It is also true that one needs other opinions of a script to be sure you are not wasting people's time with frivolous scribblings. So I want to thank Cher Cadd, Dave & Kris Nelson, Harold Antrim, and Edith Campbell for their excellent input.

I would also like to acknowledge Branden Buerkle for his artistic work on the cover of the book.

Chapter 1

THE BEGINNING

It was a solemn occasion, sitting at the breakfast table of the President of the Philippines. It was 1957 and we had been invited as part of the evangelistic team of a crusade being held at the famous Sunken Gardens in downtown Manila. Evangelist Dr. Bob Pierce was the speaker and the Four Flats Quartet the featured music.

But the solemn occasion was not solemn for long. As usual, and as was expected of this musical foursome, we began singing our trademark "sugar stick" - De Animals A'comin', a hilarious story of how Noah put the animals into the Ark. President Magsaysay cracked up, as did the other invited guests, waiters and more servants. We sang a number of other songs, but entertainment just seemed to come to us naturally.

"What am I doing here?" I asked myself. "Is this some kind of omen?" How could I possibly know that in a few short years I would come back for the next 32 years of my life in this country, living among the people, having breakfast with several more presidents? But that's another story.

The Four Flats Quartet started in a peculiar manner. Not many people believe this, probably because it is so unbelievable. We were all students in 1946 at Pacific College (later to be renamed George Fox College) in Newberg, Oregon. At that time the college was small with about 100 students, and fervently evangelical. Under the leadership of Professor Roy Knight, whom we affectionately called "Pop," the college sent out musical groups to represent the school in various churches around the Pacific Northwest. We were not sure just what Pop's job was. He usually picked up whatever needed to be done, such as ordering food for the dining hall or building new buildings, but his main role was being "Pop" to the men of the male dorm. One day Pop announced that all who were interested in singing in a quartet should gather at Woodmar Hall that night.

He was probably as surprised as I was when about 40 or more fellows showed up. My first observation was that it wasn't organized very well. Pop suggested that we all get together in groups of four. He didn't seem to care much whether one could sing or not, nor whether there might be the four distinctive parts that are needed to make a musical foursome. At any rate, everyone seemed to find

1

three other male species with whom to harmonize. I began to see that this was turning into something like choosing up sides in a baseball sandlot with eventually that unwanted guy left in last place. And that's just how it turned out. There were four guys left over that nobody seemed to want. You guessed it; they were destined to become "The Four Flats."

As with all quartets, the personnel changed from time to time. I don't really remember who was in that original group. I'm not even sure that I was one of them. At any rate, after a few weeks it shuffled down to what became a fairly permanent quartet. We named ourselves "The Four Flats." We have often been asked why we chose that name. Our usual response is, "It refers to our billfolds."

Ron Crecelius was the second tenor (usually singing the melody) and had a cultured and beautiful voice. He came to Pacific from the military service, having spent the war years in the Air Force. It was immediately following the close of World War II, so our campus was overflowing with veterans. His gregarious personality and his hilarious sense of humor made him extremely popular on campus. He would prove to be one of the quartet's great assets that branded us as not only singers, but performers as well.

Norval Hadley sang first tenor and came from Albany, Oregon. Norval had a great sense of humor too, as we all did, but he had leadership qualities and was a good student. He was too young to have been in the military. Norval became student body president in his junior year and I was his vice president. He distinguished himself in many ways, particularly by winning the Oregon State After-Dinner Speaking contest.

Many a night in Hoover Hall (the men's dormitory) you could hear us practicing. As young college students, we were most interested in how much fun it was to hear close harmony coming out of our vocal chords. To grab hold of a juicy barbershop chord was actually exhilarating. The crazier the song the more we were attracted to it. Norval had been to several Methodist summer camps and he always had an abundance of hilarious, if not slightly odd ball, renditions of "camp songs." One song was called <u>Beans</u>. We put together our own arrangement and it stayed in our repertoire all through the years of our association.

Harlow Ankeny came to the group a little later with a smooth lyrical voice. He had an uncanny ability to pick out the baritone part with ease. We seldom used any music. It was all put together by ear. We each seemed to know just what our part should be, and the closer the harmony the better we liked it. Harlow brought with him a sense of business too. He had been editor and sports reporter for his high school newspaper so, with his typing skills, he was a natural for doing our correspondence.

I hardly knew why I was in college. After I finished my term in the US Navy during WW II, I was just wandering. Coming from a poor family, it never even occurred to me that I would go on to college. When a former high school friend asked me to attend a banquet with her I had no idea it would be at Pacific College. I heard I could attend this school on the GI bill and that interested me. It seemed to be the right thing to do. I've had a life-long interest in music, sang the lead in our high school musical and had played percussion in the Camas, WA High School band. The vocal music teacher saw some potential in me and in my senior year she even sent me to Portland for voice lessons from her own private teacher, at her own expense. This led to a vocal solo for my high school graduation. Through all my younger school years my parents were never able to buy me a musical instrument so the school drums and vocal music became my primary interest. Sitting next to my father in church, I automatically picked up how to sing bass so I was well prepared when the quartet came along.

The quartet had really done very few performances except for clowning around at some college events when our choral music professor, Roy Clark, suggested to us that we enter a barbershop quartet contest to be held at Forest Grove, Oregon. It was the first year of an event that would be repeated annually for more than 50 years, and is no doubt still going to this day.

We had never sung barbershop before so we looked up some numbers in an old book I found and for the first time we were forced to read music. That didn't last very long because we discovered that barbershop chords came quite naturally to us. Once we got the swing of it, we were making up our own chords and arrangements.

As I remember, we only had a few weeks before the big contest. Professor Roy Clark was drilling us and helping us with the harmonies, picking out parts on the piano. His encouragement kept us going and helped take away some of the apprehensions we had about entering a competition in a field in which we had no experience whatsoever. No doubt there would be professionals entering who would make us look like the amateurs that we were. Self-confidence was not our forte.

To make matters worse, at the last minute our baritone at the time, decided he could not do it and keep up his grades too. We considered backing out. How could we find a new baritone and ask him to catch up on all the rehearsing and memorizing that we had done in the past weeks? There was only one solution. Roy Clark was our only hope. Surprisingly, he was not reluctant to pinch hit. After all, he had rehearsed these numbers almost as much as we had. (Secretly, I believe he was envious of this opportunity to sing barbershop.) Of course, he could sing any part except possibly bass. He had a keen ear for music and was educated in music harmonies. He was our man.

+ + + + + +

When we arrived in Forest Grove for the contest we were overwhelmed by what we saw. Someone had turned back the clock to the Gay Nineties (1890's). The whole town was dressed in period costumes. Even the stores had been decorated to look the part. Men were sporting long-handled mustaches; women were in long dresses and bows. Everything was turned back to another century and, of course, the quartets were asked to be in costume as well. Not being able to afford to dress alike, we decided to take on different characters of former days. We managed to find a couple of flat straw hats, a vest or two from the college drama closet, and we painted on some false sideburns. I had fun as a cop with baggy pants, suspenders and a real London type Bobby's helmet. Norval was dressed to look like Abe Lincoln. We were a motley looking crew, but we would pass in the maze of other colorful characters.

The closer we came to performance time, the more nervous we got. This was big time entertainment and though we had a natural bent, how would we do before a large crowd under the pressure of an important contest? We really didn't know much about authentic barbershop tradition. We only knew we enjoyed singing together and had lots of fun in the process. As the time drew near for the program to start we decided we could not do this in our own strength so we went down stairs backstage, found an unoccupied room, and bowed our heads together to pray. We told the Lord that this was our gift to Him and that He could do whatever He wanted with us. We just wanted to be His.

As the program began we could see that we were up against experienced barbershop balladeers. Fortunately we were back stage and didn't get the full impact, but with each quartet that came to the stage our nerves grew tenser. Finally, it was our name, "The Four Flats," being called. There was no turning back, so we charged on to the stage.

We had chosen a song we discovered in a very old book. It was an arrangement of <u>Oh You Beautiful Doll</u>. It was impossible for us to sing without adding a few antics, which usually came to us quite spontaneously. It was never necessary for us to plan out the choreography as most musical groups do; if it didn't come naturally it always seemed awkward and stilted. So we probably broke barbershop tradition by tossing in a bit of humor, as was our style. At any rate, the crowd went wild and we won the first prize of 100 silver dollars, quite a sum of money in those days. The officials crowned us the "Barbershop Champions of the Pacific Northwest."

The stage erupted into a mass of humanity; people coming for autographs, flashbulbs going off, pushing and shoving and general pandemonium. Finally the official photographers from the Portland Oregonian newspaper managed to call for some kind of order and began setting up the stage for photographs of the champions. Little did we know that this would cause a stir back in the halls of our beloved alma mater.

Out came the cancan girls in their Gay Nineties flapper outfits. They surrounded us, some even sitting on our laps! We could see that Professor Roy Clark was going to have some explaining to do when he got back to Pacific College, the evangelical Quaker college of the West. His face turned red as a beet, but there was little we could do but accept the adulation and attention that this event had thrown upon us.

Next day the Sunday Oregonian printed a special magazine edition that featured the Forest Grove gala event and, of course, there we were, The Four Flats in several photos. The main large photo included the cancan girls and it looked for all the world like Roy Clark had his arm around one of them.

Thus began a period in our lives that none of us had anticipated and no one could have guessed how dramatically it would affect the rest of our lives.

———————————————

Helen's Comments…

Dick Cadd, legally known as Richard G. Cadd—bass of the Four Flats Quartet and my husband. Of course, he wasn't my husband when the quartet first started. I had always stated, "I don't need a tall, dark, and handsome man—he just can't be short and red-

headed." Well, Dick is both short and has red hair! However, I couldn't help but be interested in the cute short red-headed bass of the Four Flats Quartet.

I'm not sure the college was ready for this particular male quartet, but the first time they sang in chapel, everyone knew there was something different about these guys—and the school was never the same!

The first time I heard the quartet and Dick's incredible singing— short and redheaded didn't matter that much. I think I fell in love with his voice first of all, and I still love his singing after more than 55 years of being married to him. However, I found there was a lot more to love than just his music. (Because Dick was short, most people thought he sang tenor.)

Even though I became sure of my love for Dick, I was still a little bothered because he was so short. If we got married and had a fight, would it make me look down on him? Could I respect and admire him as much as if he were taller?

One night GOD taught me a lesson. It was as genuine as any experience I have ever had and changed my entire way of thinking. I seemed to be standing on a platform looking over a vast crowd of people. At first it was hard to distinguish any one person. The LORD said to me, "These are people whose height is according to their character." As I began to look more closely, I noticed the variety of very short to extra tall. Suddenly I saw one man who was taller than all the others, and I realized it was Dick. In the Bible GOD says, "Don't judge by a man's face or height...I don't make decisions the way you do. Men judge by outward appearance, but I look at a man's thoughts and intentions." GOD gave me the privilege to actually see Dick and be aware of what was genuinely important. Dick is truly tall to me and I love him with no reservations.

Last Visit with a President...

Error!

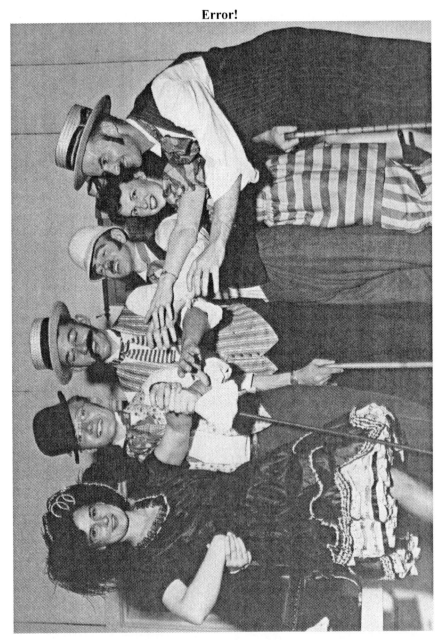

Barbershop Champions of the Pacific Northwest

Chapter 2

THE CHAMPS

Suddenly, we were famous. We didn't want to be, but we discovered that along with winning the barbershop ballad contest came a certain notoriety whether we wanted it or not.Actually, it wasn't so bad. We began to get requests for singing engagements that far surpassed anything we had done before. And on top of that we were getting paid big money. That was great for the two in the quartet who were not veterans because it helped pay their school bills. Chris and I found ways to spend ours as well. Since we were both married we had other expenses.

Since Professor Clark had a full time teaching job, he really didn't have the time or the inclination to be running all over the Northwest singing. It was time to find a replacement. This is when Harlow Ankeny stepped into the picture. Our voices and personalities blended and that foursome, Chris, Harlow, Norval and Dick began a singing career that would last full time for over 15 years.

The engagements were piling up and it was often late at night by the time we had driven home from towns and cities that were 50 to 200 miles away. Weekends were always packed with engagements at churches and youth meetings. Things got especially wild toward the end of the school year as Youth for Christ had their year-end special banquets and party nights. We would just hop from one to another in what seemed a never-ending string from town to town. Our program provided plenty of hilarious fun combined with a spiritual punch that made the night a good Christian alternative to the high school Prom. We were young enough that we appealed to these high schoolers and yet old enough to bring a serious note. Just what YFC was looking for.

When June rolled around that year we received word from the city of Forest Grove that they wanted the quartet to ride on the Forest Grove float in the Portland Rose Festival Parade. We would represent their city as the Barbershop Champions of the Pacific Northwest and the competition, of course, was the big event that they were determined would be their claim to fame for years to come.

What could we say? Since we were the champs of the very first contest year there were no others to do this promotion. Now June in Portland does not necessarily mean summer weather. And as it happened, this parade was on a very rainy day. The Forest Grove float was beautifully decorated and even had a barber's chair on a raised platform in the back. Chris was put in the chair and Norval was pretending to be the barber. Harlow and I stood on each side as we sang our way through 10 miles of parade route. It hadn't started raining until just as the parade began. To add to an already messy situation, we discovered that the decorations and frills the committee had given us to wear were made of some kind of red colored paper. As the rain began to soak through our clothes, we later discovered the colors went right on to our white shirts underneath. We had multicolored underclothes when it was all over.

Nevertheless, as good sports we warbled on our way with the only barbershop ballad we thought to be appropriate on this special occasion, "It Looks like Rain in Cherry Blossom Lane."

That school year ended in exhaustion from this wild schedule. By now, Pacific College began to realize that they had a public relations gold mine in their midst. We were asked if we would travel the summer representing the school in camps and churches across the country. Being young and full of energy, not to mention the headiness of our new found fame, it seemed like a great way to spend the summer. So the next few months were spent singing in churches and camps throughout the Midwestern part of our country recruiting young people for Pacific College. And they came. It was probably the largest increase in enrollment that the college had ever known other than the increase by military veterans following WW II.

It wasn't long after we had won the barbershop championship that the college also realized the Four Flats had called attention to this tiny Quaker school as nothing ever had. Unfortunately there were several colleges on the West Coast that had the word "Pacific" in their name as well. Often when the quartet was introduced at a program the MC would say that we were from some other Pacific college, especially Pacific University at Forest Grove, Oregon. After all, that is where the contest was held and they had a "Pacific" too. The confusion continued for several years until finally our school decided to change its name to George Fox College (now George Fox University). Of course, there were other factors involved, but the attention brought to the school by The Four Flats was no small influence.

By the time 1948 came around, we were deep into a semi-professional singing career. Though we were still in school, we were constantly on the move with singing engagements. By February the Forest Grove Barbershop contest was upon us. The committee insisted that we had to return a second year to "defend our championship." At least this time we knew a little of what we were getting into. As the contest loomed, we were more prepared. We had abandoned our ratty original outfits and had purchased new flat straw hats just like the Gay Nineties. By now we had a couple of suits and jackets alike so we felt we had come up in the world.

Nevertheless, we were not too cocky about winning. In the original contest we had met and observed some fine barbershop singers; groups like The Harmony Vendors from Tacoma, Washington, and The Agony Four from Oregon State College who had placed second and third respectively the year before. We were not at all sure of retaining our championship crown.

Once again, backstage in the auditorium we committed our lives and our future to God. We told Him that if winning this contest would bring glory to Him we would dedicate our talents to Him. With that said, our nervousness left us and we went out to have fun. And fun we had. Probably the fact that we enjoyed singing together so much was apparent to the audience. In a way, we were able to draw the audience into the spirit of hilarity that we were creating for ourselves.

This year we had more than three barbershop songs in our repertoire. We'd had a whole year to improve our barbershop skills so we did feel a little more confidant. I don't know where we picked it up but the song that stole the show was probably "Never Throw a Lighted Lamp at Mother." The audience went wild as we hammed it up with a tiny lamp in my hand and a kerchief over Norval's cowering head. Whatever the reason, I'll never know, once again we were awarded first place in the contest. We still had the title, "Barbershop Champions of the Pacific Northwest."

―――――――――――――――――――

Helen's Comments...

As young as the quartet guys were, they always attracted girls. Remember how girls used to swoon over Frank Sinatra and scream for Elvis Presley? It wasn't quite like that, but sometimes when we went with the quartet, we were amazed as young girls swarmed around our men and fought for their autographs.

It wasn't always easy and glamorous to be married to "famous" traveling husbands. We spent many nights and weekends alone.

Until we began going with them, our summers consisted of picking strawberries and nursing our sore knees and lonely hearts. But at least we had each other.

Mary and I attended the same church in Nampa, Idaho and became best friends while still in grade school. Our friendship only increased as the years went by, and since Mary lived miles out in the country, she often stayed with us during the school week. We practically lived together from Junior Hi thru college days and married guys in the same quartet.

Since three of the wives were from Idaho, we sometimes went there to visit our parents. We all had older cars, so the guys taught us how to change tires, check the radiator for water, and anything else they could think of. However, it was always the unexpected things that went wrong—like a broken fuel pump. But then we were young too, and help always seemed to arrive just in time. We never had to change our own tire or replace a fuel pump!

Once the quartet became popular, they were invited for more singing engagements than they could take, so they always had a full schedule. One day Dick had a dentist appointment to have a wisdom tooth removed. But it wasn't a normal wisdom tooth –it had come in sideways. The only way they could remove the tooth was to break it up and chisel it out a piece at a time. It was extremely painful and the swelling looked like Dick had a baseball in his mouth. The Dr. gave him some pain pills—I called them "happy sex pills." Dick felt so good, it was scary. He wanted more and more of the pills, so I finally flushed them down the toilet. However, even with looking like he had a baseball in his face, Dick still had to sing that night with the quartet. They seldom missed an appointment.

Forest Grove Rose Festival Float

Chapter 3

NEW NAMES

It really wasn't hard to get singing engagements now. With the barbershop title for the second time and all the newspaper publicity that went with it, our phone was ringing day and night. Of course, there were people who saw a golden opportunity here and wanted to exploit it. We had already done well as our own agents, with Harlow at the typewriter scheduling the engagements that were now coming with no effort on our part. Nevertheless, it was not long before an agent in Portland approached us about doing our secular bookings. Harlow would continue to schedule churches, but Norm, the new agent, would take care of most secular engagements.

One of the first things Norm wanted to do was change our names. Looking to the future, he suggested "stage names" so that when we became really famous our names would be easy to remember by the public. Harlow Ankeny would become Hal Kenny. Norval Hadley would be Norm Hadley. Ron Crecelius would be Ron Celius, Dick Cadd would remain the same. How much simpler could you get?

It worked out well in the beginning. Norm was good at getting conventions, radio and television, civic clubs and numerous other events that wanted some entertainment. With our barbershop title to impress them, they were lining up to get us for an engagement. Unfortunately, even though we had cautioned Norm, we found ourselves in nightclubs and other places where drinking and carousing was going on and, as Christians, we did not want to be associated with those kind of places, not to mention the reflection on our Quaker school. We cautioned Norm once more and for several months he got the picture.

One day Norm called with excitement in his voice. He had the deal of a life time for us. Bob Hope and Bing Crosby were coming to Portland for a program in the largest stadium and we had been chosen to sing on this program with them. Furthermore, it would be broadcast nationwide on radio, which would give us national attention. Norm was certain we were being launched into stardom.

When Norval shared the news with the rest of us, we were pretty high too. Our minds were reeling with thoughts of moving to Hollywood, adjusting to further fame, and how to handle all this in light of what we wanted to do with our lives.

There was just one catch. We had to tell Norm that golden night was already scheduled with a little church in Salem, just 22 miles away. We had made a commitment some time ago. This was a serious conflict.

Not to Norm, it wasn't. "Cancel it. Schedule it some other time. Do what ever you have to do to get out of it." "We'll have to pray about it, Norm," Norval told him over the phone. "Well, get back to me quick." was the reply.

Nothing like this had ever happened to us before. Somehow, a dark cloud seemed to settle over the whole proposition. Norval got us together and explained the situation. "We need to pray about this." We all agreed. We were in one of the classrooms at school so we drew a few chairs together and got down on our knees. There was silence for a while. We were each trying to formulate a prayer that would sound pious enough and yet allow us to do the thing we really wanted to do – take the golden opportunity. But none of us dared to express ourselves. God was working in our hearts. Words would not come.

Finally, after a long silence, someone said, "Why are we doing this? We know what we ought to do." Everyone agreed. "Norval, call Norm and tell him we're taking the little church in Salem that night." Right!

That day was a turning point for all of us. It was a decision that would change the course of all our lives forever. We had come to a crossroad and were forced to make a decision on whether we were going to serve God or go for the gold; the gold that was offered us in the world of fame, popularity and fortune. We had to decide once and for all time what was most important and we were choosing to follow God and give Him back the talents with which He had so blessed us. We would never turn back.

Helen's Comments...

It was very important for each couple to find what GOD wanted in our lives. Probably the most significant thing Dick and I did when we were dating, was to pray together. (We had a few interesting times otherwise—like running out of gas in the gravel pit, and then climbing thru a window because the doors were locked when we got back to the dorm. Dick never had enough money to fill up the gas tank—just enough to get by for the day.) When Dick asked me to go with him to the Prayer Room to pray together—early! before classes!—I was really excited. At first it wasn't the prayer that excited me, but the chance to spend a few more minutes with Dick. However, we soon discovered that our relationship with each other became much more meaningful when we included the Lord.

One thing Dick didn't mention about himself was that along with school and the quartet, he was also Newberg Youth for Christ Director. This was before we were married and I really liked Dick by now. Whenever he asked me to go with him somewhere, I jumped at the chance. He began asking me to go with him to the Youth for Christ rallies—and one particular night almost ended our relationship…the piano player didn't show up!

When I was in high school I learned 2 very difficult classical piano numbers. Unfortunately, they were the only 2 songs I could play— but they were so impressive everyone thought I was a good pianist. What people didn't know was that I couldn't even sight-read a simple song in the hymnbook—and I never once tried to play by ear without music. Dick led singing, and he was fantastic as he proceeded from one song to another and taught new choruses. But when he insisted I play for him that night, it had the same effect as scheduling me at Carnegie Hall. I emphatically declined, but he was desperate and convinced I could play anything. My hands became paralyzed, my brain went numb, my heart thumped wildly and my lungs refused to get a decent breath. I honestly don't remember much more about the meeting, but when I got home I cried myself to sleep and vowed I would never speak to Dick again.

One major problem—I was hopelessly in love with Dick and afraid he was thru with me. So the next day I secured a large hymn book, proceeded to the music hall, and practiced for hours. I memorized, sight-read, and made my first attempt to play without music. Dick's belief in me continues, and he still encourages me to do the "impossible."

Champs again...

Chapter 4

DOUBTS

A great load had just passed away. I didn't realize it and I think it was the same for the other guys, but I had been wondering where all this fame and fortune (for us, at the time) would lead us. The thoughts of a career in the entertainment world had passed through my mind many times, but I always had a lingering feeling that there was something more that God had for me. Still, music was the most important thing in my life next to God and my loved ones. And the greatest thing I could think of was spending my life making music.

My thoughts turned to the time in high school when I played percussion in the high school band. My parents could not afford to buy a musical instrument and the school drums were free, so I plunged into them with all my might. I had a natural sense of rhythm. Even there the showmanship in me began to blossom. I didn't just pound the drums, I used all the flare and fancy twirling I could dream up. Our school was chosen to march in the Portland Rose Festival so I finally had my chance to show off to my heart's content. I would like to think that our band was chosen for high honors because of the showmanship of the drum section.

By the time I was a senior I had a job working nights in the local Camas Paper Mill so I could buy my own set of drums. Buddy Rich and Gene Krupa, the greatest drummers of that day, became my idols. To play in a dance band was my goal. To my astonishment, one day I was invited to join the high school dance band. All the members were the elite of school society, the sons of doctors and lawyers. I felt far out of my element since my Dad had always been a simple farmer. Nevertheless, I was thrilled at the chance to be on my way to my goal. Some years later, my widowed mother and two younger siblings decided to move to California from Camas, Washington, where we lived. I did not want to leave school and the dance band I had just started playing with in my senior year. I would turn the radio up on to the loudest dance band I could find and then proceed to accompany them on my own set of drums. The neighbors had little appreciation for my added accompaniment.

My father died when I was 14. My mother had tried her best to raise us in church and we followed somewhat reluctantly. But by this time I was really not interested. I was definitely going astray. Our little Friends Church in Oak Park was about to have an old fashioned "revival meeting." Mom had begged me to go. I promised I would, but I put it off until there was only one service left. That's not a good maneuver. The last night of a revival meeting is usually the hottest. And so it was.

I remember almost nothing of what was said that night. The invitation was given to receive Christ but I was holding on. Then from out of nowhere an arm slipped around my shoulder and there was my former Sunday School teacher. He was a godly man, and he said just the right words to melt my hard heart. "Dick, if you'll give your heart to Jesus tonight, He will make something good out of your life."

That shot right to my heart. I had just recently picked a note off my car that said, "Young man, if you don't start driving more sanely in this neighborhood you'll have an occasion to see the police." I was a juvenile delinquent and I knew it. In fact, I was a bit proud of it. That night was a great turning point in my life. I gave my heart to Jesus and I've never been the same.

The next day there was an ad in the local newspaper. It said, "ONE TRAP DRUM SET - FOR SALE." I knew I had to get rid of the drums. They were my idol that would take me down the wrong road. At that time the only use for drums was in a dance band and I knew that the great drummers of those days were usually drug addicts. I could easily see myself going that way too, since I wanted so intensely to be the best.

Then came the enemy of my soul, whispering doubts in my ear. "Now you've done it. You've sold your drums and you'll never amount to anything." Little did I know then the plans God had for me, musically and every other way. He did not take music out of my life; he only changed the tune.

Now here I was back at George Fox College. Once again facing those familiar doubts. How could I forget all that God had done in my life? He took me through the war years safely, even fighting in the greatest naval battle of history, the Battle of Leyte Gulf. God had kept me with a Christian testimony through these years since high school and provided a college education which I had never dreamed possible. Why would I ever doubt that He was going to give me the best life possible?

Helen's Comments…

Dick said he had doubts, but I always thought he was very strong in his relationship with the LORD. I mentioned my doubts about his height and red hair, but my vision of him took care of that problem. He also had other qualities that were very convincing.

From 1ˢᵗ grade, it seemed like I always had a "boy friend," so I had some very good comparisons for Dick. One of my boy friends in high school took me for a ride in the country on a beautiful day— sunshine, no pressure, and totally relaxed. But we had a flat tire. His reaction was anger. By contrast, Dick and I were coming home from a meeting in Washington on a cold, rainy, dark night. The meeting had gone longer than we planned, and we were late getting back to the college. We were afraid I would be locked out again, and had decided no more climbing in windows. And then we had a flat tire. Dick calmly got out in the cold rain, and with a flashlight changed the tire. When he finally got back into the car, soaking wet, I expected him to be very upset—but he wasn't! It was simply a problem that had to be fixed, and he proceeded to fix it—no big deal!

This has been the story of Dick's life. Whatever needs fixing, he doesn't fuss and fume and get angry—he just goes about fixing it. This has made my life (and the lives of our children) much easier, pleasant, and fun.

Chapter 5

WEDDING BELLS

After we agreed together that the quartet ministry was God's leading for us, there were practical things to be done. By now, we had all completed our college degrees and were each married. Chris and I had married before we finished college and had lived in the notorious "Vets Housing" on campus. These houses were made up of the old military barracks from Camp Adair which were torn down and reassembled by students under the direction of Pop Knight.

Chris chose for his partner a petite little blonde from Portland whose parents were hard working farmers from the old country of Austria. Divonna Schwietzer knew how to work, for she often did the chores, working hard along side her mother and father on the family farm just at the edge of Portland. She always had a beautiful flower garden wherever they lived. The day after they were married Chris and Divonna left at noon for a quartet engagement at Sheridan Days, a celebration in a nearby town. Some honeymoon! Such were the quartet days.

Harlow had also married a farm girl. Gertrude Haworth was from Star, Idaho. Her family was active in the Friends church of Star and she knew the hard work of a farm as well. Gertrude was involved in many aspects of college life and was the perfect match for Harlow.

Norval and Mary McClintick had been dating all through their four years at college. It was a joke around school that Mary and Norval had always been boy and girl friend – perhaps from birth. Everyone knew they would marry, but they waited until their Senior year. This was because they had no GI Bill like the veterans had. When Norval and I were running for president and vice president of the student body our junior year, Mary and Helen were our biggest fans. They even made up a political commercial jingle and sang it all over campus. They even made a recording of it and had it played incessantly, driving people out of dormitory lounges. (We won anyway.)

It seems that Norval was the butt of a lot of our jokes and mischief during those days. Now we knew the date that Norval and Mary had chosen to be married well in advance, because they did not want some quartet engagement coming into conflict with their special day.

Armed with this valuable knowledge our devious minds went to work. The plan, eventually agreed upon, was to conjure up a fictitious engagement for the quartet that none of us could resist accepting. For a little authenticity, while in Portland one day Chris went into the New Heathman Hotel and helped himself to a letterhead of the hotel along with one of their printed envelops. Using the impressive stationery, Harlow and Chris created a masterpiece. It was from a certain J.C. McCloud. He was supposed to be a banker from California who was passing through Portland and heard about the famous Four Flats Quartet. There was to be a banker's convention in Seattle, Washington, beginning with a breakfast meeting the 17th of December. Would we be willing to come and provide the entertainment? Of course, it just so happened that the 17th was the morning after Norval and Mary's wedding in Oregon.

On the way to an engagement one night, Harlow pulled out this letter and read it to us all. Of course, Chris and I were duly surprised right along with Norval. Norv got this really sickish look on His face when he realized the conflict with his wedding date, but when he heard that the bankers would pay us $1000 for our efforts (more than any of our engagements had ever paid), he began to think seriously about it. And of course, he realized, as we had planned all along, that if we took it, we would need to drive all through the night of his wedding, in order to get there in time.

This put Norval in a really bad spot. If he refused, the rest of us would miss out on all that badly needed money. And having just gotten married, he needed the money too. When he began praying about it the rest of us began to wonder if we'd gone too far.

I remember the next engagement a few days later. As we gathered in the car the big question was, "Well Norval, what have you decided about taking the offer from J.C. McCloud?" To our utter astonishment, he said he would do it. It would be hard, but Mary had agreed to drive to Seattle after the wedding where they would belatedly begin their honeymoon after the banker's convention. There was silence in the car. We hadn't expected or prepared for this turn of events.

Finally, Chris took the letter of acceptance which Norval had already prepared and started tearing in into little pieces. I only wish I had a photograph or a video of Norval's face at that moment. It was a picture of horror, astonishment, disappointment, anxiety, confusion, frustration and rage all rolled into one. Over the years, and even to this day, we often refer to J.C. McCoud with a roar of laughter. It was always an inside joke for many years that only the four couples got – until now.

Norval and Mary's wedding was memorable for us all, not only because we all attended the solemn affair, but because the other three in the quartet could not let this occasion pass without having some fun. Afterward the three of us followed the honeymooners. It was late December and very cold outside. Their chosen place for the night was surrounded by puddles of water from recent rainy days, which on this frigid night were now frozen. Our plan was to quietly sneak up to the window and sing some romantic barbershop ballad. However, I had broken my leg playing football and was on crutches so the others were, of course, concerned about me trying to walk on ice with these two sticks under my arms. Suddenly there was a yelp and a crash! To my surprise, I was still standing. It was Chris whose perfectly good feet both shot into the air at once landing him flat on his back. Our sneaky surprise was no more and we all scrambled to get out of there before they called the police!

Helen Antrim and I were married in September of 1947, two years before we graduated. This was made possible by the G.I. Bill which offered to pay all veterans expenses through college. And Helen's father, who was in the ice cream business, generously continued to pay for her schooling until she graduated. Helen was a redhead, same as I, and I never imagined getting serious over someone whose temperament might match mine. She was a cheerleader and editor of the school yearbook, but the thing that really attracted me was that she, as I, had played in a high school band.

We first met on a choir tour to Tacoma, Washington. Professor Clark loaded everyone in cars at the college to take us to meet our bus for the long trip. There were three people late, but the rest could not wait any longer, so Roy asked me if I would stay and bring the late ones in my car. Yes, it was Norval, Mary and Helen. There were only four seats left on the bus, and of course, Norv and Mary sat together. That left the two remaining places for Helen and me. This was the beginning of our life long friendship. The following year's choir trip to Tacoma we were engaged. And by the next year on the Tacoma trip we were married and the following year Helen was pregnant.

After graduation, one of the practical things to be decided was where would we live during this period of our lives? It so happened that we heard from a church member that there was a house for rent in the Portland suburb of Milwaukee. It was quite large, too much for one couple so Helen and I approached Norval and Mary to see if they might be interested in renting it with us. This way our wives would have company when the quartet had to travel, which would be often. Mary and Helen had grown up together as children, went to grade school, high school, and college together, and then married guys in the same quartet, so this was made to order. Norval and I were the best of friends, had been student body officers together and, of course, sang together for years. It was the perfect set up. The other quartet guys found good situations as well.

During the next year the quartet was hired by Youth for Christ and was constantly out singing, with occasional stops back home for a few days in the Portland area. We were paid $200 a month each, if we raised it in offerings.

+ + + + + +

I'm not sure how we met Bob and Bernie Gorman, but they were a very young couple who had moved to Portland from Kansas and knew no one in the area. They had no place to stay and very little money. We had plenty of room in our house, so we invited them to stay with us until Bob got a job.

Things went along great. While Bob was out looking for work, Mary worked days at a local bank and Bernie was great company for Helen and our baby. Bernie was expecting a child so Bob desperately needed work.

Finally, Bob was offered the job as Youth for Christ director of a rally in Richland, Washington. He would drive up there to see what it involved. Though his car was old and needed repairs, he made it there.

That same weekend Bernie went into labor. The quartet happened to be home so Helen and I rushed her to Vancouver to our Christian physician, Dr. Brougher, who had delivered our baby, Carolyn.

All seemed to be going well after the baby was born, although it was a hard birth. Bob came back to visit, but had to return to Richland for a rally. The doctor said everything was fine. The quartet had to leave for meetings in Tacoma, but Helen and Mary visited Bernie every day. One day the phone was ringing as they entered the house after their visit. It was the hospital. They wanted to know how to get hold of Bob. Something had gone terribly wrong and Bernie was dying.

Panic took hold as the girls frantically tried to call Richland to find Bob. He was miles from Vancouver, probably two hundred or more and his car was unreliable. Nevertheless, when he got the phone call, he left immediately for Vancouver. Along the way the car broke down and by the time he arrived at the hospital, Bernie had died.

The next few days were the most difficult of our lives as we passed through the valley of the shadow of death with our friend Bob. Helen and Mary, who had by this time been caught up in the lives of this precious couple, experienced enormous grief. Bob took Bernie's body back to Kansas and left their newborn baby with us for the next several months. Helen nursed both the newborn baby boy and our own six month old Carolyn during this time. The quartet returned home, canceling engagements for this emergency.

After a few days it was necessary to go back to Tacoma where we were in the midst of evangelistic meetings. We were so young that we did not know how to cope with such sorrow. In the host home where two of us were staying, they had a recording of Jack Holcomb, a prominent gospel singer of the day, singing "There is a Balm in Gilead." I played it over and over again. It was the only thing that seemed to soothe my grief.

"There is a balm in Gilead to make the wounded whole."

Helen's Comments…

In the beginning, each member of the Four Flats Quartet was single. Over a period of years, each member married the girl they met in college.

Chris and Divonna were the first to get married, and although they were ahead of the rest of us in college, they still had a year to go after their wedding. Divonna really was small and cute, and I think Chris fell for her the first time he saw her—even tho' many of the girls had their eye on him when he walked onto the campus. Divonna had a beautiful soprano voice, but unfortunately, she was the only one of the wives who didn't come from Idaho. So she didn't make the trips with us to Idaho when the guys traveled all summer, but usually stayed with her parents outside the Portland area. However, we often stayed in Newberg in our vet's houses, and depended on each other for emotional and physical support.

Sometimes it pays to be late—since that's really the way Dick and I began our relationship. Although we had no choice about sitting together on the bus trip to Tacoma, we deliberately chose to sit together on the way home.

The quartet stole the show every time they sang. The choir members enjoyed them as much as the audience. I became more impressed with Dick and since Mary was already going with Norval, it seemed natural for me to date one of the other quartet guys. Mary and I did just about everything together.

I remember Dick telling me how he was going to date a girl for a year or two before getting engaged. And then he planned to be engaged for a year or more before getting married. He also told me that he was never going to tell a girl he loved her until he knew he wanted to marry her. All of this was very interesting to me and I had thoughts of upsetting his plans. When we really began going steady, I decided he would probably ask me to marry him at the same time he told me he loved me. But it was Norval who told me that Dick loved me—before Dick got around to it. And Dick didn't propose the same night he told me he loved me. His proposal came several weeks later as we were sitting on a log at the beach.

We were married the same summer as Chris and Divonna. Their wedding was soon after school ended in the spring, and ours was just before school started in the fall. We hadn't really decided to get married that year, but when both Dick and I attended a conference at the beach in Oregon, we decided we couldn't wait. By the time I got home to Idaho, we only had about 2 weeks before our proposed wedding date, and I hadn't even talked to my parents about our plans. I don't know why, but I was afraid to tell my Dad we wanted to get married—in 2 weeks! We didn't have a lot of choice on dates, because school was starting soon.

The day I arrived home from Oregon Dad said we were going to our cabin at Payette Lakes (about 3 hours drive into the mountains). We went to the cabin without my telling them. The next day we went across the lake in our boat and Dad got out to see someone. I finally found the courage to tell Mom, and then asked, "Will you please talk to Dad?" She replied, "Absolutely not! You tell him yourself!" As soon as Dad came back to the boat, Mom informed him, "Helen has something to tell you!" I had no choice but to blurt out that we wanted to get married in 2 weeks. Dad turned to Mom and calmly announced, "You owe me a milkshake!" He always made "bets" with milkshakes—and he had bet my Mom that if I went to Oregon for that week, I would come back with wedding plans. So we immediately went home to Nampa and prepared for the wedding. Both Dad and Mom were wonderful and totally efficient—and we actually got married on time. (My Dad was always on time!)

Since both Chris and Dick were veterans, we could live in the vet's houses. There were several units—each with 4 houses joined together by common walls. This made for interesting living since our next door neighbors could almost knock our dishes off the table by hitting the wall. With walls thin enough to put your fist thru, conversations were rarely private even in your own home.

One day we decided to put on a show for the neighbors. Dick hit the chair with his belt and I screamed, "Don't hit me again!" However, if we got upset with each other, it was better not to talk until we could go someplace in the car. Our first years of marriage adjustment were pretty public.

Norval and Mary waited until their senior year to get married, so whenever Norv didn't get enough to eat in the dorm, he came to our house and ate our stale leftovers. We were convinced he didn't have any tastebuds, but he was handy to have around.

One day during our first year together, Gertie (who later married Harlow), came to see me at an unusual time of day. It took her a few minutes to work up the courage to tell me that Dick had been hurt in football practice, and had been taken to the hospital. At that time the hospital was in an old house. When I arrived there, I found that Dick's leg had been broken. It was a very serious break because he had kept running on it after it broke. They had to wait several days for the swelling to go down before the Doctor put a steel plate in his leg. Dick was awake throughout the whole operation, but when they wheeled him out, I took one look at him and passed out. Then more waiting for the cuts to heal before putting on a cast. All of this meant the quartet had to cancel singing engagements—but eventually Dick could go with them again. Fortunately, the cast didn't interfere with his voice.

However, the cast did interfere with Dick's driving and it suddenly became my job to be chauffeur. One memorable day I managed to get us into the middle of a parade in downtown Portland. Nobody could figure how I did this—but Dick nearly died of embarrassment— and he couldn't even scoot down out of sight because of his cast.

Norv and Mary finally got married. They had gone together longer than the rest of us and they knew they would marry, but they didn't have the financial help like the veterans had. Dick has already told the most memorable part of their wedding and honeymoon. We still talk about it when we get together and we still use the name "J.C. McCloud."

That left Harlow as the only single quartet member. Gertie was from Idaho, and although Mary and I were from Nampa and Gertie was from Star, we had met when our youth groups got together at times. All of the quartet and wives were convinced that Gertie was the perfect mate for Harlow—even though he seemed slow in recognizing this fact. However, with six "cupids" at work, he finally got the message. They were married a couple of years after our wedding—on the same date. Since Harlow and Gertie were a year behind the rest of us and needed to finish college, they missed out on the Alaska trip.

After Dick and I were married, we still had 2 years of college before graduating. We both majored in music—Dick for the right reason and Helen just to be in the same classes with Dick. We were required to give a senior recital, so we wanted to make it a joint recital. Dick sang and I played the trumpet. These recitals were usually given at the end of the year, but we had a problem—I got pregnant early in the school year. After consulting with Roy Clark, we changed to a much earlier date and decided not to tell others until after the recital. (But I'm pretty sure people guessed!)

The quartet was scheduled to travel for the college that summer, but they arranged to be home three weeks before our baby was to be *born and stay until three weeks after she was born. However, she didn't cooperate and refused to be born until the day the quartet had to leave again. Dick was here for her birth, but had to go immediately afterward—leaving me when I needed him most. This was all part of being a "quartet wife."*

Living together in a big beautiful furnished house in Milwaukee with our best friends seemed perfect—except that our husbands were gone most of the time. Since I had a baby I couldn't take a job away from home, but Mary worked in a bank. We met Bob and Bernie Gorman when the quartet was home for a few days. They had just moved to Portland from Kansas and still hadn't found a place to live or a job for Bob and Bernie was pregnant. So it seemed ideal for them to come and live with us. We often needed a man around when the guys were gone, and I liked the idea of having company when Mary worked all day. We had plenty of room and became very good friends.

Bob wasn't around when Bernie had her baby, but he rushed home as quickly as possible. Both Bob and Bernie were excited about his new job as Youth for Christ Director for the "Tri-Cities" in Central Washington. As soon as the Dr. assured him Bernie was fine, Bob went back to Washington to look for a home for his family and to lead some weekend rallies. The last night Mary and I visited Bernie in the hospital, we found her sitting up, feeling great, and excited about coming home.

It only took us about 30 minutes to drive home from the hospital, but as we walked in the door of the house the phone was ringing. We were shocked with unbelief when the Dr. bluntly told us, "You must find her husband immediately; she can't possibly live more than a few hours." Unfortunately, the hospital found Bob before we did, and told him it would be good if he could come back because Bernie was having some trouble. But they didn't make it sound urgent at all. However, Bob left immediately for home, but his car kept having flat tires and other troubles.

Before Mary and I went back to the hospital, we made a phone call to Bob and Bernie's pastor. He agreed to meet us at the hospital. When we got back to Bernie's room, everything had changed. Now there was frantic activity with nurses racing in and out. We couldn't go in, although they did let the minister in to speak with her for a few minutes. He told her we were there. This was a new experience for Mary and me; a nightmare from which we couldn't awaken. We sat in the hallway watching, waiting, praying and crying.

About 11:00 p.m. we became aware of the doctor standing before us, looking tired and haggard. He spoke softly, "I'm truly sorry. We did everything possible to save her."

We really couldn't comprehend what had happened, but managed to ask, "Why? She was fine a few hours ago!" The doctor patiently explained, "I know. I thought she was out of danger. She had a very hard birth and vomited while being administered the anaesthetic. It didn't come all the way out and instead went into her lungs which caused a poison gas to form and fill her lungs with liquid. She actually drowned, but we call it double pneumonia. We've been checking her constantly and thought she no longer had a problem."

Mary and I were dazed and sick, and knew we couldn't face Bob, so their pastor said he would stay and meet him. The quartet guys came home immediately and stayed as long as possible to help Bob in every way they could. Bob left for Kansas and it would be several days before I could pick up Bernie's baby from the hospital, so our husbands decided Mary and I (and our baby) should go to Tacoma with the quartet for a few days.

The quartet had to stay in Tacoma, but we needed to get back home—Mary to work and Helen to pick up Bob and Bernie's baby boy (Bobbie). On the way home Mary and I smelled smoke. We pulled over to the side of the road, grabbed Carolyn, and jumped out of the car just as the whole underside of the dashboard burst into flames. Someone going by had a fire extinguisher and someone else ran across the street to a service station to call for help. I don't remember how we got home that night, but we were totally drained— emotionally and physically.

I picked up baby Bobby, and nursed him along with Carolyn for several weeks. My mother came out to help me take care of the two

The Four Sharps

Divonna Schweitzer   Gertrude Haworth

Helen Antrim   Mary McClintick

Chapter 6

THE WILLIS SHANK

Toward the end of World War II Torrey Johnson, Billy Graham and a few other dynamic young men started a new movement called Youth for Christ (YFC) and it was catching fire all over the USA and abroad. Portland had one of the most active and exciting rallies in the country directed by Dr. Frank Phillips.

Dr. Phillips was a veterinarian, but evidently found a better and higher calling when he learned about Youth for Christ. He remained the Portland YFC director for many years. Dr. Phillips had three teenagers who were all active in their local YFC Clubs and Bible Quiz Contests. Dr. Phillips built the Portland Saturday night rallies to the point that they were held in the Civic Auditorium, the largest in the city. Thousands of teenagers would gather on Saturday nights to hear great Christian music, Bible quizzes, singing and a fast moving evangelistic message.

Our quartet began getting invitations to sing at the Portland rallies. In fact, we sang there so often that we were considered regulars and developed a close relationship with Dr. Phillips. During this time we were also singing for many other YFC rallies around the Northwest and in California. The Four Flats were featured at the annual International YFC Convention at Winona Lake, Indiana. When we were in the Midwest we would usually sing for rallies in the Chicago, Detroit and surrounding cities of the area.

During one of our engagements at a YFC rally in Seattle a middle-aged man came up to us after the rally and began a conversation with us. We discovered that he was a ship captain. At the time, he was refitting a World War II minesweeper to convert into a vessel with a medical clinic and small chapel on it. Would we be interested in joining him for an evangelistic cruise up the coast of Canada to Alaska? We were a bit skeptical, but it did sound exciting. We would pray for God's answer.

Harlow was a year behind the rest of us in school and he wanted to finish his education the next year. The trip would take a whole month. It was difficult for him to give up an opportunity like this, but in the end, Harlow really felt he had heard from the Lord that he was to go ahead and finish his senior studies at George Fox.

All well and good, but what were we to do without a baritone? God provided by bringing a young man who had a natural ear for the baritone part and knew a lot of our music from hearing us sing for several years. Randall Emry was from Greenleaf, Idaho, and was well known to us as a fellow student at GFC.

Randall had a pleasant personality with a winning smile and a great sense of humor. A sense of humor was a must in this group, because we spent a lot of time laughing. Most of our humor was spontaneous, making a joke out of almost any situation. There were times when I wondered if we carried it too far, but then, I realized it was the glue that held us together for so many years.

We met Captain Stabbert and the WILLIS SHANK in Seattle on a sunny day in April, 1950. The ship was named after Willis Shank, a Youth for Christ leader who was killed in an airplane crash on a high mountain in Alaska just a year or so before. Though we had never met him, we had heard many stories of his exciting life.

The captain, his wife, Roberta, their teenage daughter and two sons lived aboard the ship since they had sold their house in Seattle in order to refit it. There was a volunteer crew, a cook and various helpers.

I was the only one who had ever had experience aboard a ship, but my navy time aboard a battleship did not prepare me for the bobbing of a small vessel such as this. Things went rather smoothly as we traveled up the Inland Passage along the Canadian coast stopping to visit small Indian villages along the way. Nothing like this had ever happened in these isolated villages so we caused a great commotion each time we pulled into a dock. Norval had brought his unicycle with him. Since there were no streets he would ride through the villages on the boardwalks and by the time he rode back to the ship, every kid in town was following him. Then we would announce the evening service and in many places, it was said everyone in the village came to our meetings. The little chapel could only hold about 70 people, packed and standing, so the overflow was all over the ship, wherever they could find a place to hold on.

The response to the quartet singing was astounding. Who would have imagined that these isolated Indian villagers would enjoy gospel music so enthusiastically? They could not get enough. No one wanted us to stop! It was always late at night before we could dismiss the crowd and they would be back early the next morning wanting more. What a joy it was to see so many of these precious people come to know Jesus as they heard the simple gospel message.

By this time both Chris and I were married and each had a child. Our wives were frightened for the babies when they saw many of the Indians spitting up blood on the decks of the ship, a sure sign of tuberculosis. From that point on, they watched those babies like a mother hen would her chicks. But it wasn't always possible to protect them. Everyone wanted to hold the cute little white babies and our wives lived in a state of uneasiness.

Often we would go ashore to meet the people or missionaries along the way. Getting ashore was not easy. Sometimes we would "walk the plank" - literally. One time the only way ashore was over a board about 8 or 10 inches wide stretched from the ship to the dock. The drop to the water below was about 15 or 20 feet. My balance was good so I carried baby Carolyn. Helen watched in terror. Since her balance is not the best I went back and inched her across – very slowly. Another time we actually had to climb a rope ladder up the side of another ship tied next to us. I had Carolyn strapped to my back. Helen and Divonna were introduced to a different type of fear for their babies.

Along the coastline the water was fairly calm, but eventually we came to the Queen Charlotte sound where we would have to cross in open sea. Cap. Stabbart warned us it might be rough and perhaps we should take some sea sickness pills to calm our stomachs in case we got nauseous. Most of us dutifully took the pills, thinking it would not be fun to feed the fish. We thought the pills would make us sleepy and we could nap our way over this unpleasant part of the journey.

But there was one thing we did not count on. Carolyn was too young to take a pill like that. She was at the crawling stage and Helen would not leave her in case she got into trouble so she forced herself to stay awake those several hours while we crossed the sound. It was excruciating as the ship rocked and swayed but Carolyn was happy as a lark and had no intention of going to sleep. So Helen struggled to stay awake and keep an eye on our baby, even though she was doped with the pill.

After several hours we had made the crossing and the waters smoothed out. It was time for dinner so we all headed for the mess hall. Helen had barely filled her plate when she slowly began to lower her head. Lower and lower it went, right into her plate of food. She was fast asleep. We had to carry her to her bed and she never moved until morning. That was one night when I was totally in charge of our baby!

Helen's Comments...

We were really excited when the guys told us the wives had been invited to go to Alaska with them. This was very unusual—we had simply stayed home while they traveled. However, I have never been terribly thrilled to be on the water. The inland passage was beautiful and I enjoyed that part., but when it came to docking the ship and going ashore, Dick's description doesn't begin to tell the story. It seemed like there was never a normal dock where people got off the ship simply by walking down a gang plank like in the movies. Dick mentioned the 2 most memorable experiences, but in my mind, the board we had to walk across seemed a block long and at least a 100 foot drop to the black water below. I'm sure Dick's numbers are more accurate, but I couldn't bear to see him carry our baby across and as for me, I think I crawled on my hands and knees. Obviously, we all lived thru it.

It was a totally new experience to be on a ship like the Willis Shank—especially with an 8 month old baby. Carolyn was an incredibly good baby—she even sang herself to sleep at night. Cap. Stabbart (or his wife), had found 2 baby beds for Carolyn and Ron Jr. Chris and Divonna's baby was only 6 months old at the time. The baby beds worked fine, except that they weren't fastened down like our bunk beds. We never had any trouble with them as long as we were in the inland passage, but it was a different story when we crossed the Queen Charlotte Sound and the open sea. Like Dick said, we were given sea sick pills to take. Since I grew up without ever even having an aspirin, any kind of medication knocked me out. And we were told later that we were only supposed to take half or a fourth of a pill—not the whole thing!

The sea got very rough, and Carolyn's bed began moving back and forth across the room and banging against the opposite wall. I knew I couldn't leave her there, so I took her into my bunk with me. She wasn't sick and she wasn't sleepy—she just wanted to play. I remember thinking, "So this is what it feels like when they torture people by keeping them awake hour after hour!" But I had to stay awake to keep her from falling from the bunk and getting hurt. I guess when I could safely go to sleep, I was "gone." I don't remember anything about that night after walking to the dining hall.

My memories of Alaska aren't all terrifying. I remember the beauty—the snow covered mountains, clear sparkling water, bluish ice bergs, glaciers, quaint little villages, friendly, loving Indian people, dedicated missionaries, wonderful people on the ship, fresh fish, and adoring audiences.

Their typical smiling presentation of the gospel is shown in the above picture of the Four Flats quartet, popular group formerly of George Fox college and now traveling with Youth for Christ.

A special "send-off" chapel period was conducted for and by the "Four Flats" quartet, famed singing group for the past three years at George Fox college, Monday, October 3 in the Wood-Mar hall chapel. Occasion for the "send-off" was the announcement the four will leave next Monday as full-time representatives of the Youth for Christ movement.

One change has been made in the group in order to keep the "Four Flats" on the road during the coming year. Harlow Ankeny, who had been singing baritone in the quartet since January, 1947, dropped out of the group in order to finish school at George Fox college this year.

Taking Ankeny's baritone spot is another George Fox student, Sophomore Randall Emry of Greenleaf, Idaho. Emry will not attend school this year. The new baritone has had several years' experience in quartet work and for the past summer has sung in the Crusaders male quartet at the college while traveling for the school. Other members of the group remain the same, all graduates of the school—Dick Cadd, bass; Ronald Crecelius, lead; and Norval Hadley, tenor.

Well-known for their entertainment in past years, having won the Pacific Northwest Barbershop Ballad contest, the group is planning to keep that type of songs to a minimum as they go into the gospel work on a full-time basis.

First meeting for the Four Flats was in a series of Youth for Christ rallies in and around Vancouver, B. C., beginning last Monday. Following that the group will go throughout the Northwest holding three-night meetings in various towns and cities of the area. Early

(Continued on Page 3)

Flats Begin Tour

(Continued from Page 1)

next year, according to Youth for Christ Northwest Regional Director Herb Taylor, of Portland, the quartet will take an evangelistic trip to Alaska. Highlight of the year's service for YFC will be a possible foreign trip to Europe next summer which would probably take them to special Youth for Christ services in such cities as Paris, Rome, London, and several other places on the continent.

The quartet finished their summer work late in August in a camp meeting in Nampa, Idaho. In the past two and one-half years the quartet has appeared in over 500 separate public appearances, sung over 40 radio broadcasts, and to nearly 350,000 people, not including radio audiences. The group has also traveled over 40,000 miles in quartet trips including several visits to the Los Angeles area, nearly every area of the Pacific Northwest and this summer an 8,000 mile trip through 18 states as far east as Indiana and Lexington.

Chapter 7

ALASKA

We woke up to a gorgeous morning of sunshine. Cap Stabbert said we were nearing Juneau, Alaska. The water was smooth as glass with a clear cloudless sky when suddenly we spotted an iceberg off to the starboard side. The visible part of it was white, but as we approached we could see the azure blue just under the water surrounding the ice. It was a stunning sight. Abruptly, racing through my mind were memories of stories I had heard about the Titanic and other ships that had gone to the bottom from getting too close to icebergs. I wondered where the rest of it was, that bigger part we could not see. Cap assured me that we were at a safe distance. I really wanted to believe him, but could he be sure? We encountered many other icebergs along the way, and I was never very comfortable, in spite of our experienced Captain's word.

Juneau is a city located at the base of a mountain so it looks like it is ready to fall into the sea. It had some of the modern conveniences like our cities to the south, but still looked more like some of the frontier cities you see in Western movies. Because of the abundance of snow in the winter, it never really seemed to get cleaned up afterward. It was fun to catch fish from the ship, but we were told not to eat them because they fed off the sewerage from the city. Never the less, Chris tried his hand at it and has a beautiful photo to show for it. One day someone brought aboard a large carton box of baby shrimp (caught in a proper place). We ate shrimp until we were sick. I had never seen so many shrimp in one place in my life before.

We were invited by missionaries to sing at various churches in the Juneau area. The wives didn't have to fear tuberculosis any more. One day one of the missionaries took us to see the famous Mendenhall glacier. Here was a glacier on the move. The ice that we were looking at was probably hundreds of years old as it had traveled slowly from miles away over a long period of time. This glacier continues to move slowly today and will be doing so for years to come.

The Willis Shank was going to stay in Alaska for a long time so the quartet took another ship back to the states to fulfill a schedule of concerts. None of us had ever been on a ship so luxurious. The

Princess Louise was a cruise ship with all the opulence anyone could ask for. I guess the most impressive thing was the dining room. Everything you could think of to eat was at our fingertips; and served in luxurious style. Since most of us came from modest backgrounds, all these grand accommodations were a bit overwhelming. This was a treat we did not expect, but made a wonderful climax to an already exciting trip.

Cap Stabbert, who already had serious heart trouble, went on to minister for many more years with the Willis Shank in Alaskan waters, as well as in South America and other places.

Helen's Comments…

Although the weather was clear and beautiful, it was still really cold. But we couldn't stay inside, so we dressed our babies in their warmest clothes, and stayed out on the deck as much as possible. The icebergs were very spectacular, but a little scary.

Dick has never been able to fish. What I mean is that he has never been able to catch fish. And as a rule, anyone fishing with Dick can't catch fish either. However, the fish outside of Juneau couldn't wait to be caught and as I remember it, Dick actually did get one (which he had to throw back because they were "unclean"). Workers on the ship managed to catch halibut and other fish, which is indescribably delicious when cooked immediately. (This was not the fish around Juneau.) I had never liked shrimp, but the fresh baby shrimp they brought us was like eating popcorn, and you just couldn't stop!

We actually went further north as far as Sitka, stopping at small fishing villages along the way. Each one gave us a different experience, and people really did go wild over the quartet. However, everywhere we went, TB was rampant. We prayed a lot for protection, especially for our babies, since everyone wanted to hug and kiss them. Carolyn always attracted a lot of attention because of her bright red hair. This was another area where we had to trust GOD for protection.

It wasn't easy to leave the friends we made on the Willis Shank. It wasn't easy for them either. Before we boarded the Princess Louise, there were many hugs and tears. As we pulled away from the dock, I remember someone on shore pulled out a white sheet or tablecloth and waved it until we were almost out of sight.

We were in ecstasy on the Princess Louise. We weren't down in the hold, but it must have been first class. Our room was a suite with a special bed for Carolyn. We could actually see out of the windows. And the meals were beyond our wildest imagination. We had menus with no prices, and they told us to order anything and everything we wanted—it was all included in the price of the ticket.

By the time we got home, all of us were completely spoiled— including the two babies.

Chapel aboard ship

Chris with his catch

Chapter 8

THE ORIENT CALL

It wasn't long after we returned from Alaska that we were asked by Frank Phillips to join Youth for Christ full time. It was never easy for us, as a quartet, to make such decisions. We each knew that whatever we decided as a quartet would not only affect us as individuals, it would affect our families too. We used to refer to these group decisions as "crossroads" in our lives. And indeed, that is just what they were. Many times they took us down unfamiliar roads and into experiences that we had not anticipated. So began a year of intense travel, appearing in schools, YFC rallies and churches.

One of the memorable appearances found us singing for an elementary school on the Oregon coast in a little town called Garibaldi. We were doing our regular program, geared for high school assemblies. Chris was doing some of his famous antics and the kids went wild. They were screaming and laughing so loud that we could hardly hear what we were singing. Right in the middle of one of our songs, Chris whispered under his breath, "I'd like to wring their little necks." We all cracked up, - but it didn't matter. They were screaming so loud, no one knew the difference. Ever since, we refer to that place as "little Garibaldis." We also learned that elementary schools were not our forte.

The year of ministry with Youth for Christ was exciting and fruitful. We sang often for rallies across the Northwest. Our journeys took us to YFC rallies in Seattle, under the direction of Don Rood, to Yakima with Tex Yearout and to smaller and larger rallies throughout Oregon, Washington and Vancouver, Canada. Even though each place had a unique rally director, they all seemed to have two things in common. First, each director was a fast driver. Sometimes it seemed that they were ready to be with the Lord and were anxious to speed up the appointment. Second, they were big time eaters. Lots of food was the order of the day, especially following a YFC rally. After being in this kind of ministry for awhile, I began to see the connection. There is a lot of nervous energy that goes into putting together any program, but especially an evening of fun and evangelism for teenagers. There is no way to adequately describe it. You have no appetite before a rally, but afterward you have this voracious need for food and relaxation. It was also a time to celebrate what God had accomplished at the rally.

At the same time we were meeting and making friends with the rally directors of Youth for Christ in the Northwest and throughout the country, we were also hearing some of the most dynamic speakers in the nation. Billy Graham, Merv Roselle, Jack Schuller, Torrey Johnson, Bob Pierce and numerous others were a part of the rallies where we were appearing. The privilege of this exposure to such great men of God as these would formulate our thinking and our evangelistic fervor for many years to come.

+ + + + + +

To increase our meager salaries we joined American Guild of Variety Artists which gave us an entry into National Assemblies where we sang for high school assemblies all over the country. We were considered professionals by now because we were receiving money singing.

Sometimes we were invited to take our wives with us when we would be in an area for an extended time. Shortly after Helen and I were married the quartet was invited to the Yakima, Washington, area for YFC and other meetings in churches. The sponsors would usually provide accommodations in homes. But this time the two couples, Chris and Divonna and Helen and I, were to be housed in a hotel while the two single guys got homes. It sounded like an exciting experience because none of us had money enough to enjoy hotels much.

Imagine our surprise when we were ushered to our room. One room—singular! One room for two newly married couples! As the bellboy left, we exploded into laughter. It did seem a bit ridiculous. Maybe they thought that we lived a communal life style as a quartet. Maybe this is all they could afford. It may have been a joke to see how we would react. Perhaps there was a mistake. After discovering that we had no other choice, we decided to make the best of it.

There was no curtain or any other way to divide our sleeping quarters. Fortunately, there were two double beds, but they were side by side. The bathroom was down the hall, but there was a small closet that we could use for changing into our pajamas. So, one at a time we accomplished it with embarrassed blushes. Divonna and Helen slept in the middle; Chris and I on the outside. There were lots of giggles before we settled down for the night.

To add to our uniqueness, Norval rode a unicycle. It made him popular at school functions and always attracted attention wherever he went. He often would use it as a means of getting noticed and then give a gospel illustration. One night at a YFC rally in Seattle we decided to use Norval's unicycle as part of the program. One man didn't like what he considered to be sacrilegious and he stomped out of the rally. He happened to be a YFC board member. Later, when we discovered the offence, we were apologizing to the director. "Never mind," he said, "We've been trying to get rid of him for years."

One of the great men of God that we came to love and appreciate was Bob Pierce. He was often the speaker for rallies in the Portland area. A great friend of Dr. Frank Phillips, Bob would come to the Portland rally often after his journeys into China and other parts of the Orient. He never failed to stir our hearts with the passion and love he felt for those in other lands. Whenever he finished his talk I literally felt rung out like a dishrag.

Bob had a liking for the quartet. I don't know whether he liked our antics, our music, or if maybe he saw in us four young men who wanted to serve Christ with all our hearts. Nevertheless, our lives were destined to be tied together with his for many years.

In 1950 Bob returned from war torn Korea to the Winonna Lake YFC Conference and invited us to accompany him to Korea. He said he couldn't promise that we would come back alive, but could promise that God would use us to bring brightness to a suffering people. We couldn't get visas and didn't go then, but God used this to bring us to a "willing to die" commitment.

At the end of our year with Northwest Youth for Christ, Dr. Phillips approached us with the idea of taking a tour of the Orient. Bob Pierce wanted us in meetings in Korea and there were others who would sponsor us in Japan, Okinawa, Taiwan and the Philippines. Again, this was one of those momentous decisions. Some of us figured the quartet would end soon and we would get on with further education and God's calling on our lives. We considered this for a long time, some having a greater struggle than others. How would this change our lives? What about leaving our wives for nine weeks? How would they manage? What about the cost? By this time all four of us were married and Chris and I had children.

After several weeks of discussions and prayer together, we came to the conclusion that this was the direction God was leading us. We had some fear of the unknown, but excitement at the same time.

We needed sponsors behind us in prayer and financial support, so we made up a promotional brochure and sent out a letter to our growing mailing list. To our amazement, many people responded and it looked like God was providing through His faithful people.

Herschel Thornburg was a fellow student at George Fox College and part time professor. He was an artist, a fabulous pianist and could play nearly any other instrument. He had a bag of "magic" tricks as well. Thinking that it would be good to have an accompanist for the quartet on some occasions, we invited him to go along on the trip with us.

The day finally came when it was time to leave. We each made our way to the Portland airport with our families tagging along for a send off. We had never taken an overseas flight so we had butterflies in our stomachs. We kissed our wives goodbye and boarded the plane. Not long after we took off Harlow discovered he still had the keys to his car in his pocket.

Meanwhile, back at the airport in Portland, Gertrude made the same discovery when she tried to get into their car. She had no keys of her own so the wives moved into panic mode. They immediately called the Seattle airport hoping to get a message to Harlow. Fortunately, we had a short layover in Seattle so Harlow had time to get the keys sent back to Gertrude. This was only the beginning of years where the wives were coming to the rescue of one another.

We flew over the North Pole in those days and we had a refueling stop at a tiny spot in the Aleutian Islands where we all got out for a snowball fight. It was a short stop and it wasn't long until we were flying into Tokyo, Japan. As we approached Tokyo I could not help but remember the last time I was there…

Our battleship, the Tennessee, had entered the harbor at the end of the war to behold a completely destroyed city. The effects of the pounding of the U. S. Airforce were evident in every direction we looked. Hardly a building was left standing. Some were still smoldering from the fires. To my surprise, the captain said that we were free to go ashore, to see the city. Victory was so complete that our authorities felt we were in no danger.

My shipmate and I were really curious to look around and see what was left of this once proud city. There was really little left to see except total destruction. We had no idea where we were going. We didn't have a map, but it didn't matter since there were no street signs left to guide us. Curiously though, we came across a little church that was still standing. It was the Methodist Ginza Church right in the former downtown area. The church was the only building in blocks that was not destroyed. There were many lean-to shacks attached to the sides of the church. Up to now we had not seen very many Japanese people, only destruction. Our curiosity finally got the best of us and we entered the church.

There we found a number of young people milling around. They were all chattering in Japanese and seemed to be having a good time. Then I spotted several young Japanese naval officers in white uniforms. We were face to face with our former enemies. As we spoke, through an interpreter, we discovered that they were Christians. For the next hour or so we rejoiced together in the Lord, sharing as brothers in Christ. It was an experience I will never forget and my mind has gone back to it over and over through the years.

When I left the church that day I began thinking how insane war really is. Here we were, Christians, in different uniforms, both loving the same Lord. A few days before, had we met, it would have been our "duty" to kill each other. What is the matter with mankind?

Now, it was like I was awakening from a dream. We were landing at the Tokyo Airport. What would it be like now?

Helen's Comments...

Because of the quartet, we did get to meet a lot of interesting and rather famous people. Of course, the men got to meet a lot more people than the wives, but we sometimes tagged along. We were proud of our husbands. They were good! Actually, they were great!! And they were fun—both on stage and at home. They enjoyed each other and their music, and managed to communicate with their audiences. They were popular, and we felt privileged to be their wives.

But people seemed to have an odd idea about the quartet couples. It was sorta like we were a community of our own. And that may have been part of the reason we were literally "thrown together"—like in the hotel room in Yakima. When Dick mentioned the beds were side by side, what he really should have said was that the room was so small the beds were actually touching each other— like one big bed for the 4 of us. The closet was barely big enough for one person to stand in, so dressing wasn't that easy. To complicate things a little, we had come back from our honeymoon for this engagement, so we really were newlyweds. Chris and Divonna had been married much longer—like almost 3 months. Later at Winona

Lake, the other 2 couples had a similar experience—but they managed to have a blanket between them.

After the fellas were on the plane and headed for Japan, we went back to our cars to go home. That's when we discovered that Harlow had taken the keys to their locked car with him on the plane. Gertie did get the keys back—but not that same day. Fortunately, we had more than one car at the airport. It seemed to be a forerunner of things to come—as soon as the quartet was out of sight, everything fell apart. Washing machines ran over, dryers quit working, toilets overflowed, the children got sick, and the cars became inefficient. Cell phones sure would have been nice, but they were still "science fiction." But we had the Lord, and we had each other.

Your Friend

Friends Church

BULLETIN

OREGON YEARLY MEETING OF FRIENDS CHURCH

THE FOUR FLATS LEAVE FOR ORIENT SEPTEMBER 4

On September 4 members of The Four Flats quartet, all graduates of our own George Fox College and members of Oregon Yearly Meeting of Friends, will board a Northwest Airlines plane for a ten-week evangelistic mission to the Orient. The Four Flats urgently request your prayers for this evangelistic crusade.

The Four Flats — (l. to r.) Norval Hadley, tenor; Dick Cadd, bass; Ronald Crecelius, lead; Harlow Ankeny, baritone

51

THE ORIENT CALLS
.... the Four Flats

Over five years ago, Bob Pierce, who had just returned from a trip to the Orient, expressed his belief that The Four Flats could be a great blessing through music and the spoken word in that area. Since that time, other invitations have come to the group. The latest and most definite came over a year ago and upon prayerful consideration, members of The Four Flats felt it God's will that they make this mission. Thus on September 4 the quartet will leave for an intensive evangelistic tour in cooperation with Orient Crusades, World Vision, Inc., Youth for Christ, International, and established denominational missions. Evangelist Herschel Thornburg, well-known in Oregon Yearly Meeting and a talented musician, will also be a member of the team. By using "Your Friend" as an open letter, The Four Flats wish to amplify the following truths relative to this mission:

"God has called and definitely opened the door for us to go. Miracles showing evidence of His leadership have been performed. We are obeying this call, and, by faith, expect to see greater miracles unfold.

The mission will be a success only as our close, vitally-concerned friends pray. We have sung to tens of thousands of people, but claim only a small portion of this number as our 'concerned' public. Can we depend upon you to back us in prayer?

This tour is being made to win souls. It is neither a pleasure trip nor a missionary survey. We expect our lives to be changed before, during and after our visit abroad. We hope to be greater channels of blessing when we return home. But our primary purpose is to proclaim the salvation of Jesus Christ in the Far East while the door remains open.

Five of us will make the ten-week tour. Our wives and children will remain home, of course. Countries to be visited include Korea, Japan, Formosa, Hong Kong, Philippine Islands, Okinawa and possibly Indo China.

We are making a concentrated effort to learn the most effective way to minister, humanly speaking, in each nation and will adjust our singing and speaking accordingly. In all of this our dependence will be upon the Holy Spirit who alone is able to bring men to repentance and salvation.

We are confident God will bless our efforts as we all pray together. We are specifically praying that God will give us opportunity to reach a soul with each dollar invested in this venture of faith. "

The talents of The Four Flats are not enough . . . Without your prayers, their ministry will be to no avail. Without your financial support this evangelistic crusade will not be possible. Souls will be reached for Christ as you pray and give. You may address the quartet as follows:

The Four Flats
P. O. Box 151
Portland 7, Oregon

Chapter 9

THE RISING SUN

Dale Cryderman met us at the airport. He was a former Free Methodist pastor who was now Youth for Christ director for Japan. Slightly balding, but with some of his blonde hair still showing; he had a broad smile and a subtle sense of humor. We would get along fine.

As we made our way from the airport back into the city and the YFC headquarters, I was amazed at the reconstruction that had taken place in the nine years since World War II ended. Of course, the industrious Japanese were out to rebuild their country under the watchful eye of General Douglas Mac Arthur, the Supreme Commander of the Far East at the time.

Dale Cryderman lost no time in putting us to work. He had prepared a schedule that was going to make or break us. From dawn until dark we were singing in schools and churches. It is the custom of the Japanese to serve tea before and after each school concert. Along with the tea, they served a delicacy we came to call "bean curd." It was some kind of mushy paste that we hadn't acquired a taste for. One day we sang in seven schools, being served tea and this bean curd before and after each concert. It was really too much. Chris and I noticed a plant nearby where we delicately and secretly gave it our refreshments, as nourishment, of course. We had to be careful that our hosts did not notice our empty cup and plates or we would have found ourselves with a refill. I have often wondered if those plants survived.

During one of our last services, we were totally exhausted. After we had sung, Dale said to the young audience, "Don't you wish you had the joy and excitement that these fellows have?" He turned and saw that two of us were sound asleep on the platform, so he added, "and the peace."

One time when we were to sing for a chapel in a Nazarene Seminary, we had already had too much tea and badly needed a rest room. When we asked the pastor where the facility was, he took us downstairs and asked us to wait in the hallway. Shortly, a number of women came running out of the room. We were ushered in while the pastor stood guard at the door. It was then that we discovered the Japanese feel it is a waste of money to build two separate rest rooms – one for men and one for women. They all use the same one – at the same time. This was true when we went on to Okinawa as well. While we were using the urinals several women entered nonchalantly, to our utter amazement. We had a lot of adjusting to do.

Another custom we had not heard of was their public baths. We would often see the buildings as we were driving to meetings. It sounded like fun and we wanted to try them, until we discovered that they were like one big bath, which they all used together – totally naked.

It was also a bit of a shock to see how they grew their gardens. The Japanese have long been known for their gardening skills and large vegetables were everywhere in the markets. We often saw big wooden buckets in the gardens and when we asked about them, we were told they were "honey buckets." When we got closer, we discovered they were the foulest smelling things imaginable. It seems that the Japanese, at that time had no sewerage system, so the human excrement was collected in these buckets and taken on wagons to be used as fertilizer for the farmers' gardens. This had an effect on our appetite for vegetables after that.

Another unique experience was speaking through an interpreter. We were assigned a young man about our ages named Goto san. He was also an evangelist who gave an invitation to receive Christ at the end of our concerts. He was an amiable fellow, but did not seem to understand our American humor. However, he taught us a lot about Japanese culture. From him we learned mostly by observation. For instance, when he had been gone for several days or weeks he would not go home directly to his wife. That would show that he was anxious to see her. Not very Japanese. Instead, he would go to the library or somewhere else before returning home. He must not give the impression that he missed his wife. For us, who were far from our wives, that was incomprehensible.

The Japanese culture fascinated us. While driving through the city on our way to schools, we would often see a festival. There were large drums carried on a wagon with men pounding away, leading the procession. Men and women, boys and girls would be dressed in many colored costumes. We learned later much of this ceremony had to do with driving away evil spirits.

Day after day we sang in schools, churches and seminaries. The schedule was grueling, until we were sent to the south. We were in the country now and we were to have a couple of free days. Dale put us in what might be called a small hotel. Actually, it was a bamboo house up on stilts. We slept on the floor, as is customary in Japan, on tutami mats. One of the normal amenities of a plush hotel like this, was a maid for each one of us. The cute little female was assigned to take care of our every need. We discovered the service included helping us undress and dress as well. Imagine our frustration as we tried to communicate, in English, that we would not need this particular part of the free service.

On one of our trips, we passed by a great statue of Buddha. It is the largest Buddha in the Far East, standing about 100 feet high. We stopped for a closer look. We were greatly impressed by the size, but were broken hearted to see so many people bowing, burning incense and giving homage to this dead and lifeless idol. It was more than we could resist. We stood on the steps just below the Buddha, facing out to the crowd below and sang with all our might, ALL HAIL THE POWER OF JESUS NAME. I don't know whether it did anyone else any good, but it sure made us feel better.

Helen's Comments…

It was always exciting to get letters from our husbands. Their reactions to new experiences were fun to hear about. However, altho' Dick wrote faithfully almost every day, it was more the telegram type of letter. He always told me how much he loved me and missed me—as well as the children. But if I really wanted to find out what they were doing, I had to go over to Mary's house and read Norval's newsy letters. Dick accused Norv of describing every minute of his day—like brushing his teeth, what he ate for breakfast, etc. Norv wrote about their experiences and his feelings of what was happening. I appreciated the fact that Dick wrote so often and that he loved me—but it would have been nice to hear what he was doing and feeling. We've often talked about his "telegrams."

Dick cannot talk about his experience at the little church in Tokyo when he went there shortly after the war was declared over, without breaking down and crying. That's when the senselessness of war hit him full force. I think it was good for him to go back to Japan with the quartet and meet outstanding missionaries at work there.

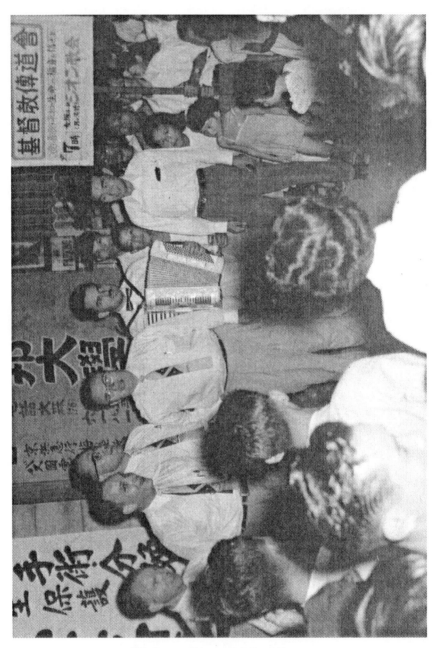

Tokyo Street Meeting

Dick in his Navy days

Chapter 10

BOB PIERCE LAND

When we landed in Korea there was some apprehension, since there were rumblings of possible war on the horizon. We understood very little about it, but there was uncertainty in the air and it was talked about wherever we went.

We were the guests of the Oriental Mission Society (OMS). They would not only house us, but were in charge of our schedule of singing engagements. Here was an introduction to real live missionaries. And how could we know that we were the guests of the legendary Kilbournes who had spent many years in China until they escaped just a few years earlier. Ed and his brother Elmer, along with their father had been run out of China when the communists took over. They lost everything they possessed—twice. Now in Korea they would start all over again.

The Kilboune boys were just slightly older than we were. They grew up on the mission field and were years ahead of us in experiences. They both had a great sense of humor so the quartet found in them kindred spirits. Ed was the treasurer of the mission so it was his job to exchange money. At the time, he could get a much better rate on the streets, so even though there was some risk in it, it was apparent that he had had some experience in the business and was not beyond the adventure. When we first arrived we were invited to a reception where everyone introduced themselves. Ed said, "I'm in charge of Black Market Finance." The father said, "I look after my son" and Elmer said, "I look after my father."

On one occasion, the quartet was to have breakfast at a missionary's house. We had all stayed in another house for the night and we must have slept late, because we were suddenly called to breakfast. None of us were ready. In fact, we were all in the bright red pajamas that someone had bought for us for the trip. Ed said, "Get going, don't make them wait." He probably didn't think we would do it, but we went into the open yard and up the outside steps to the apartment upstairs - in our pajamas. We startled the whole neighborhood. Five Americans in wild red pajamas running around like idiots. Everyone knew we were in town.

Korea was Bob Pierce country. Everyone knew this dynamic man who had come to Korea many times before. He became a war correspondent so he could stay with the Korean people through their crisis. In fact, he knew government officials and had set up an orphanage program that supported hundreds of orphans all over the land. Bob had a generous heart and was known far and wide for helping missionaries around the world and especially in the Far East. We had heard his story often about when a young missionary woman first thrust an unwanted child into his arms in China and said, "What are you going to do about this?" He gave her the last $5 he had in his pocket, urged her to take the child and promised to send more. That was the first of child sponsorship and now World Vision supports thousands of children around the world.

One day we went to a large school where they were having a whole day of athletic events, races, etc. Bob was the honored guest. He always seemed to have the right words for the moment and was so gracious when he was honored. On this occasion, he would be the one to pass out the prizes for the young students who had won races.

Bob Pierce was a man of intense prayer. We often heard that he spent whole nights in prayer. One night in Japan we caught just a glimpse of this man's passion. We were with him in a hotel room and he was literally sprawled out on the floor, face down, crying out to God. In our years with him, we often observed how he could be talking to you one minute and the next minute he was praying to God, – not missing a beat. It was so natural for him to talk to God that he just included Him in normal conversation. He was a missionary statesman for our time. He was one of a kind; one of a century. His influence on our lives then, and up to now, can never be measured.

His influence on others was also immense. Harry Holt was a simple Oregon farmer. When he heard Bob speak one time on the condition of orphans in Korea, Harry was so moved that he sold timber from his farm and started his own orphan program. While we were in Korea we ate at a missionary home where Harry Holt and about 30 orphans were quarantined with measles downstairs. When we went down to see them, these little ones were so starved for love and affection that they literally clung to us. Just to hold them and show a bit of love was so moving to us that we never got over it. Outside, Bob and Harry were making a movie to be shown on American television, which was a bold step in those days. Movies shown in churches would draw a crowd more than any other feature. Bob Pierce was a forerunner in this media field and produced a number of outstanding films over the years.

Bob had started World Vision just 5 years before. This is a missionary organization that specializes in taking care of orphans, especially in the Orient. Bob had other interests as well. Bob could not bear to see a missionary without the necessities that he needed in his work. Bob would often tell the missionary, on the spot, that he would have a new truck or an airplane before long. He would say this without talking to anyone on his board about it. He just knew that the need was there and someone had to help. Later, he would often get into trouble with those of his organization who wanted to keep him in check. Bob was the one who had the compassionate heart and the vision. He was fortunate enough that he had men who would keep him accountable, however.

Many times while we were in Korea, we would sing at Young Nok Presbyterian Church. It was the largest Presbyterian church in the country, holding about 5,000 people and quite an evangelical church as well. I remember the feeling I got as we walked along the outside windows on our way to the front platform. The smell of Kim chi (a mixture of garlic and fermented fish) was so overpowering wafting out the open windows that it nearly overcame me before we made it to the front of the long church.

There is one thing that will always impress me about the Korean church. They had a five o'clock prayer meeting every morning of every day. You could see long lines of people headed for prayer each morning. No wonder they have one of the most vibrant churches in the world today.

Helen's Comments…

Events can become a kaleidoscope of memories running together with no time frame. We know things happened, but they have no specific date in our minds. Somewhere in the quartet history, each of the guys had another job. I know Chris and Norv both pastored churches for a while—and Dick taught school in Idaho. Harlow worked for the college in public relations, but he was usually involved in some kind of publications.

When Dick and I lived in Idaho, it seemed like my husband was commuting quite often to the Portland area in order to sing at some engagement with the quartet. On one of our trips, Dick discovered that his driver's license had expired, so we decided I would have to do most of the driving. But while we were still in Oregon, my driver's license also expired. This created a big problem, because we couldn't get an Idaho license while we were in Oregon, and we had to get back to Idaho. So we drove as carefully as possible, but just outside Portland, we were pulled over by a policeman. We couldn't imagine what we had done wrong and figured we were in real trouble. But he didn't ask for Dick's license—he asked for the registration. Then the cop said, "You will probably be stopped all along the way, because a car just like yours was stolen and headed this direction." I think we were stopped one more time, with the same results.

Then during the summer months the quartet would travel across the country. The wives began going along with our husbands on some of these summer trips. I'm not quite sure where all this fits together time wise.

But as far as their trip to the Orient is concerned, it was a highlight of their singing together. And there is no question about the vision Bob Pierce imparted to the fellas. I remember Dick writing home from the Philippines and saying, "If you and the kids weren't there, I wouldn't come back." But we were "here," and Dick did come back for several more years.

By this time all of us had children—I think it was 10 between the four couples. Most of our children had someone in one of the other families that was almost the same age. It was very interesting—and loud—and fun, when we all got together at the same time.

Bob Pierce as the "charitable father"

Holt lays a foundation

Chapter 11

AMAZING MEN

We landed at Okinawa on a cold foggy morning. I was almost as nervous this morning as I was the day we first landed in Japan. I could not keep the war time memories from flooding back to my mind.

The Okinawa battle was on an Easter Sunday morning. My battleship, the USS Tennessee, opened fire on this island in 1945. It was the last stepping stone on our way to Tokyo in the closing days of World War II. I will never forget the feeling on that Easter Sunday as we were at battle stations and we were opening one of the box lunches the galley had prepared for us. There was a colored Easter egg! I was in shock for some time as I thought of the irony. Here we were supposedly celebrating the resurrection of our Lord, while at the same time bombarding this island to smithereens. Needless to say, I had no interest in eating the egg.

Later that day, we received the report that Ernie Pyle was killed on the beach that morning. Ernie Pyle was probably the most famous war correspondent of that age and was dearly loved by all who read him. He had a great sense of humor and managed to work his humor into all of his reports. As a cartoonist, he saw humor in everything around him.

But it was time to put all that behind me and try to act normal, as if I had never been there before. We were being sponsored by Overseas Crusades, a young and dynamic mission of youthful men. Bob Shelton was the director who came from a large Baptist church in Michigan. He was a gifted speaker and we heard that he was being asked to return to his home church to take over as pastor from his aging father. He certainly was qualified, but it would also be a great loss to the mission field.

There were several young men who had returned as missionaries after the war was over. Another outstanding man we met while there was with the Navigators. His name was Bob Boardman. Bob had been a marine during the war and was shot through the throat. He had no vocal chords left and could only talk in a raspy whisper, but his testimony was so interesting and his love for the people was so evident that in spite of a tremendous handicap he was leading people to the Lord.

In the same mission were two other young guys, the Denler twins. They were fine musicians; Gene played the trumpet and Dean played the trombone. They would each get on the front fender of a car or truck as they drove through a city, playing their instruments and gathering a crowd for a meeting. The quartet had a great time with all of these men as we used music to gather crowds and to tell them about Jesus.

Bob Shelton's wife was pregnant and about to deliver any moment, so he was keeping a close eye on her. Sure enough, before we were to leave she ended up in the hospital. It was a U.S. G.I. hospital located in a quonset hut. I don't know who suggested it, but the quartet was asked if we would stand outside her window and sing to her. Dutifully we found our way to the hospital and discovered that it was impossible to tell what room she was in from the outside. We made an intelligent guess and started singing. As I remember, we were singing in the women's restroom window. I couldn't help but recall the time we tried singing outside Mary and Norval's window on their wedding night. That didn't work so well either.

One night we were invited to a home where Dawson Trotman, the head of the Navigators, was to speak. The host asked us to sing. That meeting was our first time to meet this dynamic man who was instrumental in influencing so many servicemen to follow Christ during their days in the military. It was the ministry of the Navigators that brought me through the years of service in the Navy. A group of Christian men aboard ship would meet once a week for a Bible study. The time together was an encouragement to each other and kept us looking to the Word of God as a beacon in an atmosphere that was definitely not friendly toward Godly things.

The Navigators had a scripture memorization course that we each worked on. Every week we would take a verse of scripture to memorize. Verses were written on small cards that we could carry in our shirt pockets. As good sailors, we were required to repeat the location "fore and aft." In other words, we had to say where the scripture was found in the Bible, before we quoted it and after we quoted it. That's a very good way to ensure remembering where to find it. The Navigators had other printed material and Bible helps that kept us going in hard times. This would not be the last we saw of Dawson.

Our time in Okinawa was truly inspiring. The young missionaries there left a lasting mark on all of us in the quartet and changed our attitude completely on the kind of people missionaries really are.

Helen's Comments…

I honestly have no idea where we got the impression that missionaries were weird or misfits or radicals or couldn't do anything else—because my parents had missionaries in our home all through my younger years, and I thought they were the most wonderful and exciting people I had ever met. But when Dick and I were in college, being a missionary wasn't "cool" and "we just weren't that type." However, our time with Youth for Christ and World Vision totally changed our minds.

I remember one Youth for Christ speaker who declared, "If GOD didn't clearly tell you to stay home, then your job is to go." "Go into all the world and preach the Gospel…" (Matt. 28 & Mark 16) We also met many remarkable, intelligent, fun-loving young people who were totally committed to sharing CHRIST with the world. We were beginning to think that we were the misfits—not missionaries. This radical change in our thinking made it possible for the LORD to lead us into mission work in the Philippines for 32 years. (That part of our lives came later) But we were greatly influenced by the amazing men and women the quartet met on their trip overseas.

Sometimes when the guys were traveling and we couldn't go with them, we went home to be with our parents. This meant I went to Idaho. Our children loved this experience—especially since my Dad owned an ice cream factory. They could have all the ice cream they wanted. Then grandpa decided to really spoil them (since we weren't around very often.) He gave instructions to all of his delivery truck drivers that if one of our children flagged them down at any time, they were to stop and give them whatever they wanted. Our boys thought this was the closest thing to heaven—and they took full advantage of this privilege and power. I think the deliverymen deliberately drove near wherever the children were playing—and you can imagine the popularity our children enjoyed. They also loved the time with cousins their age.

We did have a few disasters. One summer it seemed like the children destroyed or damaged everything they touched. It wasn't malicious, it was just childish things. One example was when Steve slashed a long hole in the outdoor couch—which happened to be plastic and couldn't be repaired. I was very upset, and when they begged to go the next summer, I informed each one that the first time they destroyed anything, we were going home to California. So the first night we arrived, I was going to drive my Mom's car somewhere and managed to totally break the gearshift off. The next day when I was making the bed, I broke the wooden frame. It had to be taken to a repair shop. Before the week was over, as I was doing the dishes, I split in half Mom's beautiful antique cut glass pitcher. The children didn't do any damage that summer, while everything I touched turned into a disaster. I decided the LORD was trying to tell me something! Adults can have accidents too!

After being gone for an extended time one summer, Chris and Divonna came home from her parent's place with a load of frozen meat that was packed in dry ice. But while they were gone, somehow the freezer had been accidentally unplugged. Since they already had some meat in the freezer, the odor was unbearable, and they never did get the smell to go away.

Quartet in Japanese attire

"The Gospel Clowns" performing

Chapter 12

THE SECOND CHINA

Taiwan had no memories for me. This was a whole new experience. Taiwan had been in the news a lot with Chiang kai chek and most of his troops escaping from Mainland China to this island fortress just a few years earlier. His wife was educated in the USA and was a dedicated Christian.

Again, we were hosted by Overseas Crusades. O.C.'s early beginnings were in Taiwan when Dick Hillis was invited by Madame Chiang Kai Chek to come and preach to Taiwan's defeated Chinese troops. The troops were disillusioned and discouraged. Dick had known the family when he was in China as a missionary, before he also had to escape the communist takeover as the Kilbournes did.

In the early days of O.C.'s history Ells Culver was one of Dick's helpers as they got started. Ells describes Dick Hillis as a humble and gifted man. He tells the story of a lesson in humility that he learned from Dick. The team had been out preaching the day before and in their travels had met with wet weather and lots of mud, so the truck they were using badly needed washing. While they were resting in their room, Dick, the head of the mission, asked if Ells would he mind washing the truck. He grumbled an OK, but didn't move. Not long after, Ells looked out the window and saw Dick outside in the yard, washing the truck.

Taiwan was wide open to the preaching of the gospel so we had an open door to schools, military bases and churches. We were sent up and down the island singing and preaching everywhere. We spent several days with some of our own Friends missionaries who had a work in the city of Taichung. Along the way Herschel got acquainted with an independent work and took on some of their support. Later, he returned to this work with his family and a truckload of musical instruments to minister for many months.

Taiwan is a beautiful island with lush greenery everywhere. The roads were good throughout the island, although so many people rode bicycles that it slowed traffic to a two wheel pace. Taiwan was sparsely populated until the hordes moved in from China so, at that time, there were two distinct people groups as well as two languages. This made for much misunderstanding, both in the government and in every day life.

There were also a number of missionaries who had come from Mainland China when the Communists took over. The Presbyterians, whose work in Taiwan is over 100 years old now, had a strong work with a seminary.

One of the workers and translators that O.C. gave us to travel with us was Bill Lee. Bill could speak not only English and Chinese, but Japanese as well. He was a small boy growing up when the Japanese occupied the island. Bill was so Americanized that he joked all the time with American humor. Of course, he was one of our favorite characters.

One of the highlights of our time in Taiwan was a visit to a leper colony. The only experience I'd ever had with leprosy was reading about it in the Bible. Seeing and talking to lepers was a chilling experience. Lillian Dickson was a short little plumpish woman with abundant energy. She was the wife of the head of the Presbyterian Seminary. Wives of Presbyterians were not considered to be missionaries, at least not in the normal sense. But Lillian was as different as anyone could be. She had worked among headhunters and mountain tribes and she had cared for these poor unfortunate people for many years. Now she was pleased to have the quartet bring some brightness into their miserable lives. To see smiles on the faces of these dear people whose bodies had been ravaged by this destroying disease was worth all the effort of the entire tour. Needless to say, we sang with compassion that day. It is very difficult to sing with a lump in your throat.

Lillian had her own private mission on the side called Mustard Seed Inc. through which she raised money to help the lepers. Bob Pierce was one of her biggest champions.

As we left Taiwan, we could see that we had merely scratched the surface of the work that was there to be done. Perhaps other missionaries having to leave China would find their way to this needy field.

Helen's Comments...

While our husbands were having lunch with Madam Chaing Kai Chek and singing for lepers and ministering to discouraged military troops, we were home trying to hold everything together—

emotionally, socially, physically, spiritually, and financially. As we kept having more children, this kept being more of a challenge.

I remember one time when I tried to save money. I bought a turkey really cheap on sale. Although cooking turkeys was unfamiliar to me, I managed to bake it. When it was finished, I took the meat off the bones and put it in several meal-sized packages for the freezer. Then I boiled all the bones to make broth. Of course, this had to cool and be strained, so it was an all day and half the night procedure. (I like to make simple, fast, and no mess foods, so this all went against my nature!) Besides this monumental task, I had children to take care of and all the other normal jobs that go with a family.

I finally got the children to bed, and about midnight I finished straining the bones to get everything I could possibly salvage from this big turkey. I filled a gallon container, opened the refrigerator door, picked up my precious broth, and watched in horror as it slid from my hands. The jar broke into hundreds of pieces, and the greasy liquid (mixed with broken glass) went over almost the entire kitchen. This included under the refrigerator and stove. I was so tired—I just sat down on the floor and cried. If Dick had been there, he would have helped, but he was gone! And it wasn't just the mess—it was the loss of the broth and all of my precious time.

After I cried until I couldn't cry anymore, I cleaned up my mess and climbed into a lonely bed.

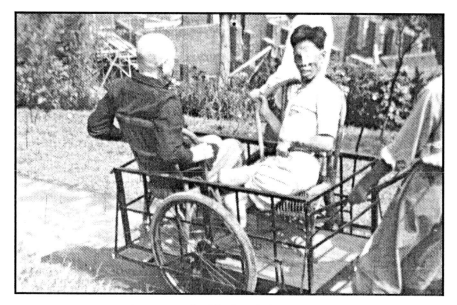

Lepers in Taipei, Taiwan

Lillian Dickson with her beloved lepers

Norval, Dick and Chris in a Peddiecab

Chapter 13

"I SHALL RETURN"

When the door of the plane opened at the Manila airport, it was like a blast of hot air from a giant furnace. Was this a normal day? It was indeed! For the next several weeks we would live in a virtual steam bath. We were drenched in sweat most of the time. The only relief was an occasional air conditioner, and missionaries were expected not to have one. (We stayed with missionary families.) The more you suffered, the more holy you were. Or so it seemed.

This was the country where General Douglas McArthur was to leave his imprint forever on this land and people when he made that declaration early in World War II, "I Shall Return."

Again, we were sponsored by Overseas Crusades. At this time the field director of O.C. in the Philippines was Ells Culver, formerly from Taiwan, and the son of missionary parents who had served in China. Ells was a fearless young man who was able to schedule us in the most amazing places. The Philippines is predominantly a Catholic country. One night the Catholic hierarchy was having a big celebration in downtown Manila, with only the most important and dignified people in the country on the program. I don't know what Ells told them about our quartet, but we found ourselves on the platform before what seemed like millions of people in an open-air meeting. The crowd was so dense that we had to have a police escort running interference for us just to get to the platform.

This was typical of our time in the Philippines. Ells had us scheduled in schools all over the country. At one point, he sent us up the island of Luzon singing at high schools all along the way. When we got to Baguio City, the town in the mountains that was "vacation land," there were schools and colleges everywhere. Coming back to Manila we stopped to sing at Clark Air Base, the main U.S. Air base in the Far East. While we were standing outside the main gate waiting for transportation one night, we observed some young Filipinos dancing and singing, just passing the time. Right then I fell in love with the Filipino people.

Downtown Manila is filled with colleges and universities, some as large as 65,000 students. In a radius of 10 blocks there are over one million students. Needless to say, we could still be singing there if we were to reach each one.

During the trip up north, we had occasion to eat a meal with a Filipino family out in the country. We were a bit skittish about the food, but had definitely been warned not to drink the water. Even though water was served we all left it alone except for Herschel our magician. He took pleasure in taunting us. As he would drink the water, he would hold it up to show us how good and tasty it looked. The rest of us held out in spite of being so dehydrated that we were miserable. When we arrived back in Manila we were glad we had abstained. Herschel was very sick for several days, and we thought we might have to ship him off to the hospital.

While we were in the Philippines, we got acquainted with several more outstanding people. The Denler twins showed up to join us on several occasions. Ells had sung with a quartet in Asbury College and three of the four were on this mission field together. Jack Stowell and Keith Brown were the other two. Jack was the second tenor and had a smooth mellow voice and Keith was their very low and deep bass. We didn't sing together much in public, but we jammed a lot at night, and whenever we were in from meetings. Jack particularly, loved to strike up a song. We all had a wide range of songs we knew and if we didn't know one, we could fake it well enough. I'm sure they all missed singing as a quartet, so even though we were tired, we joined in with them in the fun of singing. Once again, we were learning what amazing people missionaries can be.

When we sang in high schools we gave an entertainment show which included imitations of famous groups and people such as Bing Crosby, The Sons of the Pioneers, The Ink Spots, and many others. Chris was a big asset here. He could impersonate just about any voice he wanted, so we could go on and on with voices. We had insane skits as well, which usually put the audience in stitches. We would always settle down to a serious note with several gospel songs and usually gave an invitation to receive Christ.

While we were in Baguio City, we were asked if we would sing for a hospital in the town of La Union, located down the mountain and near the sea. It was a small hospital owned by one family and headed by Dr. Macagba. Each of the family members were involved in the hospital. The wife and son were also medical doctors and the two daughters were pharmacists. We struck up an immediate friendship, partly because we were about the same ages as the son and daughters. We even found time to go bowling together. We were certainly surprised when we got to the bowling alley. We found that they have something called "duck pins" which are a similar shape as ours in the States but very much smaller. There are even fewer in a row and the ball you throw is more like the size of our softball. It was very easy to throw the ball right between the pins. Needless to say we were not the champs.

When we left LaUnion, the whole hospital staff (and it seemed like half the town) came outside for a photo together and gave us a lavish sendoff. In later years, the younger Dr. Macagba joined World Vision as part of their medical team, working in various parts of the world.

As we were preparing to return home, we paid little attention to our passports until we got to the airport. Then we definitely had to present them in order to get on the plane. All went well, except that Norval could not find his passport anywhere. He began unpacking his luggage. Nothing. It was getting close to the time for departure. The rest of us were behind a wire fence ready to board the plane, looking at Norval and wondering if and when we would ever see him again. Then all of a sudden Hershel said, "Well look here!" There in his camera case was Norval's passport. No one ever figured out how it got there, but Hersch tossed it over the fence and Norval was rushed through all the stations, in what could be called United Airlines all time record-breaking send off.

As we spent time in the Philippines, we noticed that the Filipino personality was so captivating that we were very much attracted to them. In one of my letters home to my wife I said, "If you weren't back there, I don't think I would ever leave here." Little did I know that I would one-day return with my family and spend 32 years as a missionary to these wonderful people.

Helen's Comments…

It seemed like the quartet was having an incredible time— meeting all kinds of interesting people and having unusual experiences. We seemed to have unusual experiences too, but entirely different from our guys. Besides appliances that quit working and cars that didn't run right, we sometimes had to rush another quartet family member to the doctor or hospital. Mary and I took Divonna to the hospital when she had their first child. We really depended on the others for support and help in every area of our lives.

Although times and dates and places might be mixed up, there are some experiences that are hard to forget. Some of our children were born in Oregon, Idaho, and California. When we began having children, we often had our babies within a few months of each other. Our daughter Carolyn came first, with Chris & Divonna's son, Ron Jr. following 2 months later. Except for Harlow & Gertie's youngest child, all of the other quartet children had someone approximately their age. It went like this:

Ankeny	*Cadd*	*Crecelius*	*Hadley*
Curtis	*Carolyn*	*Ron, Jr.*	
Robin	*Jonathan*	*Dianne*	*David*
Scott	*Stephen*	*Rodney*	*Marilyn*
Paula	*Yvonne*	*Denise*	*Marcia*
Lyn	*LuAnne*	*Robin*	

Since most of the children had a counterpart in one of the other families, they always had a friend to play with. They always knew there was something special about their relationship. They were a different kind of family, but they were family.

All of us, wives and children, lived for the day when the quartet returned from their travels. The trips to the Orient were longer than usual, so to make the time go faster, I always tried to work on some project that would take longer than the time they would be gone—and try to finish it before they returned. That way the time seemed to go by faster. Once my Mother came to stay with me, so I worked a few hours each evening in a small coffee shop after the children were in bed.

Another time I learned to sew—sort of! (It never really "took," but it did keep me busy trying.) I finally learned to make a few things with a pattern as long as it didn't need to be altered in any way and if I could finish it in one day. I recall one dress I made and finished sometime in the middle of the night. When I tried it on, it was too tight. I had no idea how to fix it, so the next morning I marched across the street to Gertie and said, "Here, you can have it." Sewing was stressful, but playing the piano was relaxing.

Eventually in California, Mary and I did substitute teaching while Gertie and Divonna took care of our children who were not in school.

There were times when I was glad I didn't know what was happening with our husbands—until it was over and they were safe. For example...Their airplane had trouble as they left Hawaii for the U.S. The plane was filled with high octane gas for the long trip to the mainland—but they had to turn back and land in Honolulu again. They couldn't do this without dumping most of the gas. This is very dangerous since a small spark can cause an explosion and blow up the whole plane. Obviously it worked and they made it home safely, but the very next week a plane doing the same thing out of New York exploded and killed everyone.

I always cried when Dick left, but then I prayed and committed him to the LORD and had peace that we were all in GOD's hands. That did not mean I didn't miss him, and I prayed a lot. But I didn't worry.

Dick   Ron   Herschel   Norval   Harlow

We'll sing at the drop of a hat!

Chapter 14

CALIFORNIA, HERE WE COME.

It was a joyous reunion as we returned from nine weeks of touring the Orient. None of us had any idea how strenuous it would be, and how painful it would be to be separated from our wives for so long. Nor did we realize how hard it would be for them. Each of them had children to care for and the inevitable breakdown of washing machines and other appliances while we were away. It was time for some rest.

A few weeks later we were back at it again. It was time to report on what God had done over the weeks we had been in ministry. Churches were anxious to hear and we were enjoying the reporting.

Now came a complete turning point in our lives. Bob Pierce was so impressed with our ministry in the Orient that he wanted us with him fulltime. World Vision, a fledgling, innovative organization which Bob headed, was then located in Portland, Oregon. Frank Phillips of Youth for Christ was Bob's business manager. Chris and I went to work in the office temporarily. Bob wanted to move the office to southern California and asked if the quartet would come on full time with him in World Vision.

Things were getting complicated. Once more the quartet was up against a major decision of whether we wanted to stay together as a quartet and whether we wanted to make a major move. It would require some serious praying and soul searching. Each of us would have to decide if this was right for he and his family. It would not be a simple, flippant decision.

Several weeks passed before each of us could say yes. Harlow had the hardest time making this decision but in the end, he said "yes." World Vision would pay for moving us all down to California, but in the meantime, we would need to make a trip to see about housing. We all went down together at the same time, including our wives. Helen and Mary were both pregnant so they were interested in finding a doctor as well.

As it happened, in those days, there were a lot of tract houses being built, which was all we could afford. We went out to the edge of town where they were building and we ended up in the suburb of Glendora, just next to Azusa. There we found homes for each of us; three of us on the same street, one a block away. Each house was about $12,000. We were warned by some people not to live too close together; we might not get along. Fortunately, we did not take their advice and we will be forever grateful. During times when the quartet was away, the wives had each other to lean on. They helped each other with babysitting each other's kids and generally looking after one another. When we were home, it was easy to rehearse and often we would ride together to Whitney studio for the radio program.

It was natural that we had various things in common. One thing we all needed was a church to attend. We found a nearby Friends church in Azusa, pastored by a dynamic young man named Mel Miller. Imagine an influx of four families overnight. He was surprised and ecstatic. At the time, Mel had decided to enter a Sunday School contest sponsored by one of the national Christian magazines of the day. Needless to say, the church won the contest with the help of a singing foursome. Attendance rose from around 100 to over 700. Mel and Wanda Miller became lifelong friends.

World Vision had a radio broadcast that was aired over 130 stations on the ABC network. Of course, Bob Pierce was the main speaker while we provided the music. Each week we would drive into the Burbank area to the Whitney studios where we recorded the program or would do several programs at a time so that when we were traveling, there would always be music available. Bob Pierce was also out of the country much of the time.

Bob thought it would be good to have excellent accompaniment on the air so he hired Les Barnet to be our pianist. We would also use the studio owner, Loren Whitney, formerly with The Haven of Rest radio program, to accompany us on the mammoth organ that he owned.

Les Barnet had been recently converted out of Hollywood. He was an excellent pianist who had played for Judy Garland and other movie stars. However, he was used to being a piano soloist and it often showed in his playing. Sometimes I felt like we were accompanying him instead of the other way around. Phil Kerr had a Monday Musical once a week where he used Hollywood celebrities, recently converted, and others, giving them a platform for their talents to be shown, as well as introducing them to ministry. We were often on the program, as were Les Barnet, Arnie Hartman the accordionist, Roy Rogers, Dale Evans and many others.

We found ourselves appearing at many places around the Hollywood area. There were a group of Christians who met regularly in Hollywood, known as the Hollywood Christian Group. Many famous Hollywood stars including Pat Boone, Roy and Dale Rogers,

Bob Bradford the ventriloquist, and many others. Singing in places like this became common.

It wasn't long before we were getting well known. Someone made a request to see us on the television show, "You Asked for It" with Jack Linkletter. We made our way to downtown Hollywood and to the CBS studios where the TV show would be aired. It was almost becoming routine and a little bit too much to handle.

During our time with World Vision we were asked to sing for many unique and exciting occasions. For instance, we were invited to go to Oklahoma City to sing for the Billy Graham Crusade that was being held there. I'll never forget that the night we were to sing was the same day that Dawson Trotman, head of the Navigators, died trying to save a young girl from drowning. The whole Billy Graham Team was in mourning and it was tough just getting through the service. The Graham team was very close to him and they all realized that Dawson was with the Lord so in the end there was joy mixed with sorrow.

While we were in New York we sang again for the Billy Graham Crusade. We got better acquainted with Cliff Barrows, who took us to various smaller meetings during the day. We just happened to have in our repertoire the song "Carolina in the Morning," which we sang again and again for him in the car as we traveled from place to place. He would say, "Sing my favorite song, boys" and we knew what he meant. He was from Carolina. Cliff was the workhorse of the team, always the first one to arrive and the last one to leave. He was often completely exhausted at the end of the day.

We traveled by plane a lot of the time, but that was not always possible because we were singing at small places on our way to New York or Washington D.C. We heard that there were funeral family cars for sale cheap at funeral homes in downtown Los Angeles. So we went down and sure enough, we were able to buy a Cadillac family car for only $350. It sounded like a fabulous price at the time and today it sounds even better!

This car would hold nine passengers so we could take our wives to engagements, driving only one car. It had a roll-up window just behind the front seat so that two of us could sleep on long trips while the other two would share the driving and keep each other awake. It was the perfect car for a quartet. Interestingly, we were criticized for driving such a luxurious car. We wanted to put a sign in the window, "I'll bet our car cost less than yours."

As World Vision's quartet, we were representing World Vision everywhere we went. We were free to conduct the services any way we chose, but we always gave people the opportunity to adopt an orphan from the thousands of orphans that World Vision had available.

Each year in February there are a group of congressmen that sponsors what is called the Presidential Prayer Breakfast in Washington D.C. Our quartet was asked to sing for this event on several occasions. Dwight Eisenhower was president the first time, and Richard Nixon on another occasion. It is a very solemn time when men and women of all faiths join together to recognize a higher power and to beseech Him for our nation's problems. It's great to know that there are men and women of God in our government who pray and meet together for fellowship and Christian concern and guidance. They have had such notable speakers as Billy Graham, Bob Pierce, Mother Teresa and others. I was greatly moved to see senators and congressmen, both Republicans and Democrats, praying together for our nation.

Helen's Comments…

Our "exploratory" trip to California to look for houses was pretty memorable. Although our husbands had traveled by air, none of the wives had been on an airplane. We were a little apprehensive, since we were all leaving small children behind. And as the plane was taxiing down the runway to take off, someone across the aisle opened a newspaper to one of the biggest headlines I had ever seen…"Two Passenger Planes Collide in Midair" "Worst Plane Disaster in History." This happened over the Grand Canyon. Both planes went down and everyone was killed. This certainly didn't help our nervousness, but it was too late to get out!

Another incident was that Mary got sick and discovered she had the mumps. She was also pregnant. So she spent a lot of time in the motel while the rest of us looked for our new homes.

When the guys were told not to live near each other, the warning went something like this, "You fellas might be able to get along with each other, but your wives will never make it." I don't know how anyone could be so wrong. Our friendship and living near each other was our survival. I still consider Mary, Gertie, and Divonna my closest friends.

By the time we moved to California, it was nearly time for me to have our fourth baby, Yvonne. Mary wasn't very far behind, so one of the first jobs was to find a doctor. We had no idea where to begin, and we didn't know anyone to ask for advice. So we got out the yellow pages of the phone book and simply went down the list of baby doctors in our area. Most of them would have nothing to do with us at this late stage, and we were beginning to think we might have to deliver them ourselves. We finally did find a doctor, but he came from a party and was drunk when Yvonne was born. He wasn't available at all when Marcia was born and Mary had a new doctor she had never met before.

Our tract homes were considered a great bargain. They had been built more than a year before and because of some trouble with the contractor, hadn't been sold so had been vacant for a year. Now they needed to sell fast, and we came just at the right time. The location was great—except for a railroad track that ran directly behind Hadley's and Ankeny's houses. Our house was just across the street and Chris & Divonna lived a block away. At first it seemed as though the train went right thru our kitchen, and all conversation stopped. But after a while, we didn't even realize the train was going past. I guess you can get used to almost anything.

We often argued about who had the loudest noise from the train. Harlow and Norv declared that the sound sorta jumped over their houses and hit ours directly full force. However, one night years later when we were selling our home, we stayed at Hadley's house and slept in their bedroom. In the middle of the night the train went by and the whole house shook. Dick stood up in the middle of the bed and shouted, "What was that?" I think he thought the LORD had returned and it was the end of the world.

Because the houses had been vacant so long, they were infested with black-widow spiders. Jon, who was about 5 years old, put his hand within inches of a big poisonous spider. It was a challenge to get rid of them—especially with small children who were fascinated with bugs.

And now about those loooooong cars—family cars from the funeral parlors in Los Angeles. They were a terrific bargain, in perfect condition, and total luxury. They were wonderful for the quartet, and it was especially nice for the eight of us to be able to go places together. But Dick decided it would be a good car for our family—which was growing all the time. I never did get used to the ordeal of going grocery shopping with this type of car, and I certainly couldn't park it except in big parking lots.

LuAnne was our 5th child, and when it was time for her to be born, the quartet guys were actually home and singing in the area. I began having a pain once in a while the day they were going to sing at Phil Kerr's Monday Musical in the Pasadena Civic Auditorium. Since I often had my babies rather fast, we all felt that I should go along with them just in case the baby started to come. Pasadena was pretty close to the hospital where I was to go. It was very obvious that I could have the baby any minute, so when Phil Kerr announced to the audience that the quartet might have to leave early to take me to the hospital, it didn't take long for people to know who I was. I did need to leave, but it was near the end of the program, so I waited until it was over but told Dick that I needed to go fast. However, I was stopped constantly on the way out with people giving me advice and wishing me well. I think Norv was driving, and he laid on his horn and really speeded, hoping a police would stop us and escort us to the hospital, but no such luck. I did make it in time—but just barely!

When I took LuAnne home from the hospital, we discovered that a child in our block had whooping cough. So my baby needed the vaccination when she was only a few days old. When the Dr. gave her the shot, she really got mad—he said he had never seen a baby that young with such a temper. When I got home from the Doctor, I went to change LuAnne's diapers and discovered that she had a big lump in her groin. We went right back and found that she had a hernia—probably broken loose by her screaming so hard when she had the shot. I was warned I shouldn't let her cry until they could do surgery, and they wanted to wait until she was 3 months old.

To say I shouldn't let her cry was like telling me to not let her breathe. But if she cried hard, the intestine would pop out and it *could strangulate and gangrene could set in very quickly. So Dick fixed a pop bottle cap in such a way that when she started to cry I could push on the cap and hold the intestine in. But I had to carry her all the time. I learned to do everything with one hand—laundry, dishes, making beds, getting meals, etc…*

We took LuAnne to Idaho to have the surgery so that my parents could help with the other children. By this time, our baby was so spoiled that she would cry whenever we put her down. After she was completely healed, we decided she would just have to cry, because I couldn't hold her all of her life. But she cried so hard she lost her voice, and I was afraid I had permanently damaged my child. Even when we went to the Philippines when LuAnne was 4 years old, she still had a low, gravelly voice. So we called her "Gravel Gertie"—from the Dick Tracy comic strip. She also woke up every hour until 3:00 a.m. and I began to feel like a hundred years old. Although she gave us some rough times, we wouldn't trade her for the world. And that is true of all our children.

Our son Steve and Rodney Crecelius often played together, and they almost always managed to get into some kind of trouble. One day they found some pitch on a tree and put it in their hair. Then they proceeded to twist the hair. Both ended up with a big bald spot that we were convinced would never recover—but it eventually did.

I remember one Halloween when the school nearby was having a special event—almost like a carnival. Gertie and Divonna took the older children to the school and I offered to take care of all of the younger ones at my house—Mary was sick. I had too many little ones and couldn't watch each one every minute. Scott had his finger in the back side of the door when one of the other children slammed the door shut. It cut the tip of his finger all the way off except for the skin on one side. I had no way of getting Gertie, but Mary got out of bed and tried to find a doctor who would come to the house. We were told over and over again that no doctor would come and we needed to get to the emergency room. I had at least 5 children (maybe 7) and I couldn't put Scott down—I had to hold his finger together. We finally found a neighbor who was home and would come and stay with the children while Mary drove me to the nearest hospital—which was in another town. Because I had held Scott's finger so long and so tight, by the time the doctor saw him, the finger was stuck back together and he just put a bandage on it. It was another time when we really missed our men!

Taking all of our children to church wasn't an easy job when the quartet was gone. Actually, it wasn't easy even when they were home. By the time I got all of the children ready, the boys usually needed to start over again. When Dick was home, he wanted to be on time. As I mentioned earlier, I was born with a faulty time clock. Dick would sometimes go to the car, and honk the horn. When I heard the horn, I fell apart—dropping dishes, spilling milk, etc. But after talking about the problem, Dick totally changed. He helped do the dishes, changed diapers, or dressed the boys—whatever needed to be done—when he was home. It didn't necessarily make us on time, but it sure helped our relationship.

One time when I had the 5 children at the evening service, Jon went to sleep. When the meeting was over, I woke him and told him to go get in our car while I gathered the other children. When I was almost ready to leave, someone came and asked me if I had lost a child. They had started home when they looked in the back seat of their car and saw a sleeping boy. Jon had walked out of the church and climbed into the first car he came to. It could have been a real disaster if the people had gone home and never looked in the back of their car. I shudder to think of the consequences.

It wasn't always easy being a quartet wife, but it really made us appreciate each other and cherish the time we had together. It's something we never forgot and never took for granted. And there were some fun advantages. One time we were given tickets to Disneyland and all of our children got to meet some of the people from Disney's television show.

Shortly after we moved to California and Yvonne was a small baby, Harlow, Gertie and their three boys took Dick and me with our children to a concert in another city. As we were coming home, a car going too fast around a curve came directly toward us. Harlow swerved so we didn't hit head on, but our car rolled over. Harlow was hurt the most, but with 10 of us in the car, it was a miracle that no one was killed.

Four Flats Join Billy Graham in Oklahoma City

Singing in Oklahoma City, Okla., this week as part of Billy Graham's evangelistic crusade are the Four Flats, famed Newberg quartet made up of George Fox college alumni.

The Four Flats, Harlow Ankeny, Dick Cadd, Norval Hadley and Ronald Crecelius, were scheduled to leave by plane for Oklahoma City Monday night, arriving Tuesday morning and to be in the oil city from June 19 through 24. Not only were they to sing in the regular meetings but also in various appearances before service clubs, luncheon and dinner groups.

The quartet also will sing on the "Hour of Decision radio network program to be broadcast Sunday, June 24. They will return to Newberg next Monday.

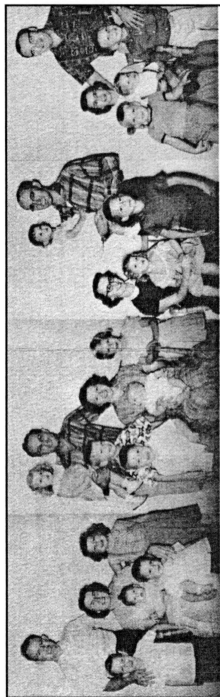

What was once simply "The Four Flats" has now become four *growing* families totaling twenty-three people!! Complete "family" portrait includes (l. to r.) Dick (bass) and Helen Cadd and four children; Ronald (lead) and Divonna Crecelius and five children; Norval (tenor) and Mary Hadley and three children; and Harlow (baritone) and Gertrude Ankeny and three children. All four families live within two-block area in Glendora, California. Each quartet member married his college sweetheart and graduated from George Fox College. Newberg, Oregon, the same year as his wife.

Chapter 15

OUR EYES ARE OPENED

People often have asked us over the years how it is that we stayed together for so long. It seems like hundreds of times someone has come up to us and said, "I used to sing in a quartet, - but we just couldn't get along." Every time I heard that said, it made me sad, and more determined that it would not happen to us.

Don't get me wrong. We had our differences. We even had our squabbles over the years, but nothing that would separate us. Each of us, having a sense of humor, contributed a great deal to our long time friendships. We respected each other for our various roles. We had no single leader in the group. Most quartets appoint a leader and that's where things often go wrong.

We each had a responsibility. Norval was the treasurer. We spotted his honesty and his thoroughness early on. One night in the very early days of our association, after a meeting in southern Oregon, we were in a motel room together. It was late and we were all tired. Norv was at the desk with the light still on and we wanted him to turn the light out but he stayed up for who knows how long. Next morning we found that he had stayed up all that time because he had lost a penny and the books would not balance without it. He would be our treasurer. Norval was also one of our preachers. With his early success as an after dinner speaker, he always had an interesting message to deliver.

Harlow was good at writing letters. Somewhere in his background he had typing and some sense of what an office should look like. He was active in writing in college. Harlow even used file folders, so we knew we had our man for correspondence.

Chris was laid back and liked to look over the whole picture. His strong point was cars and preaching. Over the years he probably owned 100 cars or more. His hobby was buying a cheap car and fixing it up. Then he would sell it and start all over again. Before long, he had to put the cars in his wife's name or register as a dealer. We often went to our engagements in one of his cars. Chris had a very unique way of preaching. He brought his sense of humor to the pulpit and his Airforce experiences too, so he always had his audience enraptured.

My job was to keep track of music, which suited me fine. We didn't always use music, but through the years we accumulated quite a collection of songs. More importantly, it was my task to give the pitches and to make out he program, with approval of the other guys. Since we were an a'Capella quartet for the most part, we had to get our starting note from a pitch pipe. We probably had one hundred or more songs to choose from and I had every pitch memorized.

So it was that each one of us had our little niche to fit into. Our personalities seemed to blend together as well as our voices. We each had dedicated our lives to Jesus and wanted to walk together as Christians.

We also wanted to walk above reproach. Being on the road most of the time, and being the idols of every teenager who came along, gave us ample opportunity to stray from the straight and narrow. It was an inspiration to be with the Billy Graham Team. They taught us so much about what it means to be faithful to our spouses and that integrity before the Lord is more precious than gold.

Often we would hear of an evangelist who had messed up his life with some woman or had been caught in financial dishonesty and it really disturbed us deeply. I found it hard to see how a Christian could think of doing such things. It was a great help to me when an older gentleman said to me one day, "The word of God is honored, no matter who preaches it." It did not make me think any more of the evangelist, but it was some comfort.

One time we were with an evangelist who always seemed a bit shady. For instance, he would have the ushers in his tent meetings bring the offering up to the platform immediately after receiving it and place it right under his chair. Other little things cropped up which made us doubt his sincerity. He had written books and was widely quoted by some of our best evangelicals. It didn't surprise us to hear, some years later, that he was shot to death in a motel room in California, with someone else's wife.

Don Lonie was a youth speaker that was straight as an arrow. Often we were booked on the same program with him. He was fun, with his dry humor, and he became very popular on the youth speaking circuit. When he discovered that there were certain YFC rally directors who had not paid us anything for singing at their rallies, he was incensed. He threatened to never again speak at their rallies if they didn't make it right with The Four Flats. Immediately a check would arrive in the mail.

One time we had a concert in a large church in southern California. It was a Sunday afternoon and the church was packed.

We put on a concert and they took up a huge offering especially for our ministry. Afterward, the pastor said, "I'll send you a check." Somehow, we didn't feel good about that, but we agreed. Some weeks later, we received a check for $15. None of us were convinced that it was the full offering amount. Again, we were not surprised to read in the paper shortly after the incident that the pastor had run off with his secretary.

The crookedness we encountered in Christian circles could have embittered us if it was not for our sense of humor. We decided to create an organization called "Christian Crooks Inc." with officers who had from time to time, cheated us out of money owed. We would appoint them to some position as officers of the organization. If someone came along who was especially crooked, we could always make him Chairman of the Board.

Helen's Comments...

We heard stories about men who traveled—who had affairs with other women and cheated on their wives. The quartet's association with the Billy Graham team made a lasting impression on them. They wanted to be "above reproach" too. This gave us as stay at home wives a confidence and trust in our husbands. The Four Flats sang for many youth groups where young girls were enamoured with them. They also stayed in homes where there were young people. They could have been tempted and even succumbed if they hadn't made a firm decision to "stay away from even the appearance of evil." I never once in my life have questioned Dick's faithfulness to me—he's never given me any reason to distrust him. This is true of all the other quartet guys too!

The guys respected each other for their different abilities. They didn't always agree with each other, but they never felt that one of them should be the leader and that's probably one of the major reasons they worked together for so many years. Of course, their sense of humor always came to the rescue. They enjoyed each other—and had fun in their programs. We also had fun when we had a chance to go with them and we never got tired of their meetings. But over all else, their relationship with the LORD and commitment to JESUS (and to their families) was most important.

One time someone decided to write a story about the quartet wives. We were interviewed and finally were sent a copy of the story to check it for accuracy before being sent to the Power Paper. We were horrified at all of the mistakes—even having me married to the wrong person. Two of the wives went to see the reporter to make the corrections, only to discover that she had already sent the story to the printer.

Les Barnett and Dale Rogers join us for a broadcast

Part 9 for May 28, 1961

CHRISTIAN Life

DOROTHY C. HASKIN

Helen, Gertrude, Divonna, and Mary enjoy
their Christian life as quartet wives

BUILT-IN PRAYER PARTNERS

Chapter 16

COVERING THE COUNTRY

Another interesting trip was to New York City to sing in a crusade in downtown Manhattan. The night we arrived it started snowing. It continued to snow the next day until it was impossible to get around. Most offices were closed since it was not possible to get to work. Because no one could travel, the meetings were canceled. We were stuck in a hotel with nothing to do, so we made our way downtown to watch some programs being aired on television.

The programs were recorded ahead of time before release. After watching "The Price Is Right," the master of ceremonies said, "If you would like to be on the show, just stay in your seat." We looked at each other and stayed in our seats. After a while he came out again with a strand of beads in his hand and began pointing to various people in the audience, asking them to bid on the beads. He immediately pointed to me as the first one. I was so frustrated that I could not think. I blundered out some ridiculous price that was the farthest from correct of anyone in the audience.

Nevertheless, I was chosen as a contestant. When I got back stage with the producer, he said to all of us, "You were not chosen because of your bid, but for your personality." I was surprised that they could see any personality from a quick bid on some beads, but I didn't argue. He went on to say that we should not hold back on our emotions, but let the excitement out. In fact, he said, "You are the show." That shot down my plan to be "Mr. Cool."

As the program went on, there were a number of items that I would have liked to win, but in the end I did win a valuable prize of $1300.00 worth of silver. It covered a large table and included candelabra, lazy susan, tea sets, wine coolers, etc. That was a lot of money in those days.

Of course, since it was pre-recorded, it gave me time to call Helen in California, and to inform Greenleaf Academy in Idaho, the school where I had been teaching. The school moved the whole student body to the gym where they could all see the program together. That was my 15 minutes of fame.

Norval was chosen for another show, but he missed the name of an important city (which we all knew) and had to settle for the consolation prize of a Polaroid camera and a board game.

We walked around town peeking in theater doors to see if there was anything going on. Norval discovered a TV show being recorded by Perry Como. At the very moment that he entered, they had stopped the show because the producer didn't like the color of the red sweater Perry was wearing. Norval had the nerve to approach him and offer the new green sweater that Mary had just bought for him. Perry tried it on and the producer approved, so Norv got on the phone and called Mary to tell her to watch The Perry Como Show that night and "see my new sweater."

Another time we were to sing in downtown Hollywood in a program which was to be broadcast over the air. There was a band on the platform as well and just as we were to go on the air as the first number to open the show, some guitar player started tuning his guitar. If you are in an a'capella quartet, you know that the pitch that you are holding in your mind for the moment you're to start singing is completely shattered when someone starts playing other notes. In the next few seconds, a finger pointed at us. We were on the air. Thanks to that guitar player we had all lost the pitch by then, and the noise that came out was in four different keys. You have never heard a worse sound!

The emcee, trying to save the day, stepped in and said, "We are about to go on the air so everybody please stand by." What a valiant effort to cover up for our worst booboo ever. It was a long time before our wives wanted to admit that we were their husbands. To keep us in our place, they bring this incident up from time to time.

+ + + + + +

Coming back from the East Coast we were driving in two cars because the wives were with us. At this time in our quartet experiences, each couple would take turns choosing a place to eat and the rest were not to say a word of complaint. We had to come to that arrangement, after years of missing meals because of indecision. It just seemed like we didn't see many places to eat driving through Kentucky. Finally, someone said, "Let's stop at the next place that has food, no matter what it looks like." We all agreed. It was getting late.

No sooner had we made the decision than we saw a run down service station that looked like it was left over from World War I. But a sign was showing that we could not miss and it said "Food." There was no turning back so we stopped the car and went in. The interior was equally as run down as what we'd already seen but we were determined to go through with our vow. We ordered from the family style menu and were served with the best down home cooked meal we had in all our travels. That day we learned that you can't always tell by the looks on the outside.

On one of our trips, we stopped to get some ice cream. We were all finishing up and Mary was slowly chewing on what she thought was ice in the bottom of her drink. Suddenly she realized that the ice was actually broken glass. She didn't know if she had swallowed any so we called a doctor. He said the best thing to do would be to eat a loaf of bread, so off we went to the grocery store. Mary took about an hour, but she finally got it down. That did it and she recovered nicely.

We had heard a lot over the years from Harlow about Allen, Nebraska, so when it became possible for us to be in the area, Harlow scheduled us to sing at his old home church. Allen was a small town. Chris said the population was 95, including the pet shop and the cemetery. Yet we were always finding people from Allen, Nebraska, in our travels. It was a Quaker community and everyone knew everyone else. It was an especially exciting time for Harlow. It came time for us to do the concert. There was a big crowd and the church was packed. During the concert we usually introduced ourselves. This time was special, as we had our wives with us. At the point where we were all going to sing together, the wives came to the platform and since it was Harlow's night, he began the introductions. He evidently was so nervous and frustrated that he reached out and put his arm around Helen (my wife) and said, "This is my wife, Helen." We all stared at him for a moment and then we broke out in laughter. The audience was in the dark, not knowing what was going on. Harlow tried valiantly to correct his mistake, while we were all wondering what the audience must be thinking. Did they wonder if we had such a close communal living group, that we didn't even know who our own wives were? What other possible things could they be thinking – and for good reason?

After we finished the introductions, we were to sing, all eight of us, a very serious number. It was a disaster. None of us could keep a straight face. We all broke up and we just quit.

Another time Friends Bible College (now Barclay College) in Haviland, Kansas, was planning a big concert and some weekend meetings and asked us to come. We decided to take the train this time. It was a pleasant journey, and we could all rest from driving. When we arrived in Haviland it was a quick stop and we got off, but our luggage didn't. Roy Clark (who was now in Haviland) was there to greet us, but when he learned that our luggage was still on the train, we jumped in his car and raced to the next town to see if we could retrieve it. We were too late. What to do next? We decided to go to J.C. Penny's store to see if we could buy 4 suits alike for the concert that night. To our amazement, they had suits to fit all four of our odd sizes. I am short, Harlow is plump, Norval is tall and Chris is the only normal size in the bunch. We kept those clothes for years after.

That night we never looked better, and no one was the wiser. However, at the end of the concert Roy Clark told the fascinating story of our adventures that day and gave the audience opportunity to help us out with the expense of our new clothes. After counting the voluntary offering at the door, we discovered the new suits were completely paid for.

Through the years we were asked to come back to the original Barbershop Ballad Contest in Forest Grove, Oregon. We were guests and not in the competition. However, some years after we won the first two contests, our wives decided to enter the women's event. They all had children but between kids screaming and cooking meals they managed to come up with two barbershop numbers. When they entered they never expected to win anything, but they were awarded third place in the contest. Little did they know that they would be asked to sing for an afterglow affair. Having only the two songs in their repertoire, there was nothing they could do but repeat the songs they sang for the contest. We were very proud of our better halves appropriately named The Four Sharps!

Sometimes our wives pulled us out of very tight situations. In New York City one time Chris got sick and we suggested that he go on to Kentucky to see his father whom he had not seen in many years. Harlow and Gertie took Chris and Divonna to the airport. We could catch up with them later. Helen and Mary would fill in. They both had heard us sing all our numbers many times over the years. They did not know everything perfectly, but we managed to put together enough songs to complete the remaining schedule in New York. When all the wives were with us we often sang an eight-part number we had known in college. Thank God for talented wives.

One of the highlights of our tours was a summer camp meeting in Liberal, Kansas. Roy Clark was the speaker and the quartet had the music. People came from all over the Midwestern states. We made many new friends during these weeks and there was a strong emphasis on missions. In fact, the Lord was so close during those days, that two of us made real commitments to go to the mission field if God would open the door. Paul Thornburg was singing with us at the time and he eventually ended up in Africa to raise his family there. I had the strong feeling that if I could not go right now, I should be willing to give an extra 10 per cent above the tithe, to send someone else. I was looking for several weeks for the one I should send. One night in Seattle after a YFC rally an old friend from college days came up to me. He was on his way to India as a missionary. Ernie Fritchsle was my man.

Even though we often took our wives with us, they were not always on the guest list for certain banquets. One night in Hollywood at one of the plush hotels where we were to sing, our wives had to wait in the lobby. This was a very special affair and we were being served squab as the main course. Just as they served us our rarely seen delicacy, we heard, "Now we will hear from the Four Flats Quartet." We left the dinner table and for the next 15 minutes we were the entertainment. When we returned to the table our squab was gone, never to be seen again. Such is the life of entertainers. However, our wives didn't feel very sorry for us. They claimed they had peanut butter sandwiches in the lobby.

The first time we were in New York City we were to sing in Brooklyn. No sooner had we crossed the bridge into Brooklyn than we saw a street fight. We parked the car and went into a cafeteria for lunch. Helen let me go through the line first so I could get my food and then hold our baby daughter, Carolyn, while Helen got her food. Just as I sat down, along came a deranged wild woman, obviously on drugs, screaming. She came over to my table and with one sweep of her arm knocked all our food on the floor. Then she went to the water fountain where there were glasses piled high and began throwing the glasses on the flour, breaking glass and shattering pieces in all directions. She was not through. Then she went up to the counter and grabbed a tray and threw it at the person serving food. From there she went screaming out the door.

The manager looked at our baby and was concerned that she was all right, so he offered to give us anything we wanted. That was our introduction to Brooklyn!

Helen's Comments…

I learned a very interesting lesson from Dick's experience on "The Price is Right." I was so excited when he phoned to tell me he was chosen to be on the show. It was something I had always dreamed of doing. But even though he won the biggest prize of the day, I was disappointed. There were other prizes I would have preferred, and the next day the final prize was much more appealing. I remember standing in the shower and wishing he had won something different. I forgot all about being excited that he got on the program at all, and that he won a big prize. As I washed my body, the LORD began speaking to me about cleaning up my attitude and becoming thankful. Isn't it interesting that the more we have, the more we seem to want? This probably fits into the category of the 10th commandment, "Thou shall not covet…"

Dick forgot to mention that when he walked off the stage after the show he was met by the New York State tax man. The prize did push us up into a higher category for taxes—we sold about half of the silver things to pay the taxes. We had silver under every bed and in all our closets—each piece carefully wrapped so it wouldn't tarnish. We kept a few major items—like a beautiful coffee and tea set—but we gave some great Christmas gifts that year.

Most of the time when the quartet traveled around the country or around the world, we (wives and children) stayed at home. But if the guys were singing in the area, we often took turns (two at a time) and tagged along. Once in a while we all went—especially after we got the long "family" car—but most of the time we were NOT invited to the banquets. We joked about eating our peanut butter sandwiches in a hotel lobby while our husbands ate gourmet meals inside the exclusive banquet hall. However, as Dick pointed out, they didn't always get a chance to eat their meal before it was time to sing, so they came out begging for our leftovers.

Divonna and I were the two wives who went with the guys to that fateful radio broadcast when they all took a different pitch to open the program. I have to agree with Dick that it was really bad. The emcee did a remarkable job of covering, but Divonna and I weren't sure we wanted to acknowledge we knew them.

When we only had the two babies, the wives and babies traveled across the U.S. with the quartet. We had two cars—each carrying two couples, one baby, and either a pink or blue potty.

Like Dick mentioned, meals became a major problem. Usually this was the noon meal, because we stayed in people's homes wherever the quartet had meetings. We were fed the evening meal and breakfast in the home. But as we traveled from place to place, we almost always ate lunch in restaurants. Eight people with eight different opinions did cause some friction—that's when we decided to take turns as couples in choosing where to eat. Of course, the couple had to agree—and once the choice was made, it was forbidden to complain.

I don't remember where the other car was, but we happened to be in the Kentucky mountains with Harlow and Gertie. We really couldn't find any place that appealed to us. I had the reputation of never setting foot in anything less than a grade "A" restaurant, and the other guys often said I had "germosis." (When we made the decision years later to go to the Philippines as missionaries, the others warned Dick I would never make it because of the lack of sanitation—but GOD did some miracles in me!) Anyhow, we drove for hours past all kinds of undesirable places. When it became mid-afternoon we were all getting tired, hungry, and grouchy! So we made a pact—the next place we came to that said "Food," we would stop and eat—no matter what it looked like. Dick told the rest of the story—a run-down gas station and garage with "Food"—and a delicious meal we still remember as one of the best we ever ate.

Two cars could be a problem, and we learned a hard lesson in communication. I think it was Baltimore where we were scheduled for a meeting—but no one told our car the name of the church or the pastor or the address. It was a big city with lots of traffic and we got separated from the other car. We had no idea if we were ahead or behind them, and there were no cell phones in those days. In desperation we pulled into a service station and parked where we could see all of the cars going by from both directions. Eventually the other car came looking for us, but we barely made the meeting. After that, we made sure everyone knew where we were going.

Carolyn had her first birthday while we were traveling, so we bought her a small cake and let her dig in. She made a terrible mess, but at least it was a celebration. One day in a restaurant, there were place mats on the table. Each mat had a plate, silverware, and a glass of water. Suddenly, with no warning, Carolyn grabbed a mat and pulled. The mat came out with all the dishes and water glass intact—staying right where they were on the table. It was all we could do to keep each guy from trying the same trick. Our two babies made friends and added a whole new dimension to our travels.

The reason Mary had to eat a loaf of white bread after swallowing some crushed glass in her milkshake was that the bread would coat the glass and let it pass without cutting her insides. I suppose if it had happened today, they would have offered her a large sum of money to keep her from suing.

People often asked if we all lived together in a big house. Sometimes they had trouble letting us be individual families. In fact, the fellas were known as "the boys," and even people they worked with didn't know their individual names. So when Harlow, in all his nervous excitement at being in his old home town, put his arm around me and introduced me (even using my name) as his wife, it confirmed in people's minds that we were just one big family. Harlow did apologize and introduced Gertie—but it's something we never let him forget! As hard as we tried to sing our song, someone would suddenly burst out laughing and then we all cracked up.

I seem to be bouncing all around memory's lane, but maybe the dates aren't as important as the experiences.

At the time when Chris got sick in New York City, we weren't terribly far from where his father lived, and that was our next destination. Harlow and Gertie agreed to take Chris and Divonna to the airport while Mary and I filled in for the scheduled meetings. We would meet the others as soon as possible. This was the summer Chris got a call from Uncle Sam saying, "I need you." (Chris was in the reserves, and there was a war in Korea.) Altho' he had a few weeks before he was to leave, we still had a schedule of meetings across the U.S. We were doing a lot of praying, and just before Chris had to leave, Paul Thornburg came to one of the meetings. The guys surrounded him after the service and asked, "What are you doing the rest of the summer, Paul?" Paul didn't have any special plans and *had been praying about what he should be doing the rest of the summer. So with one night to ask the LORD'S guidance, by morning Paul and Leona had their answer—and agreed to join the quartet just as Chris and Divonna had to leave.*

The next summer Chris was still in the service, so Paul and Leona traveled with us again. By now Divonna had her baby girl, and the rest of us were pregnant—Helen, Mary, Gertie, and Leona. We all had baby boys within a few months of each other.

One of the most embarrassing experiences of my life happened that summer when the quartet sang for a big Sunday afternoon rally at Winona Lake Campground. The guys had an engagement at a church in the area in the morning. We were staying at a hotel in the small town near the campground. When we left for the morning service, it was very hot and humid weather, so we opened all the windows as wide as possible.

We went directly from the church service to the campground. Billy Graham was speaking and our husbands were singing. Suddenly, without any warning, it started to rain—not just a little rain, but the biggest downpour we had ever seen. We remembered the open windows in our hotel rooms, with our open suitcases directly underneath. Since I had the keys to the car, I was elected to go back and close all of the windows. By the time I reached the car, it was a full-blown cloudburst. We were used to Oregon rain, but this was different.

Although I managed to park directly in front of the hotel, and only had to run the width of the sidewalk, it was like I had gone swimming. The hotel lobby was packed with people getting out of the rain. I rushed up the stairs toward our rooms, totally forgetting I needed keys from the hotel desk. I should mention that I looked very pregnant and I had a lovely rayon maternity dress on. (Rayon in those days was a rather new material and nothing like now!)

When I realized I needed the keys, I started back down the stairs, but had a funny, tight feeling. I looked down and my dress was shrinking. By now my underslip was showing about 6 inches beneath my dress, and it was getting hard to breathe. I looked awful, but I had to go back in front of all those people and get the keys. When I got to our room, closing windows didn't seem nearly as important as getting out of my dress which was trying to strangle me. It was a fight, but I finally managed to struggle out of the dress—which by now would have fit a small child. Needless to say, I could never wear the dress again and I still do not like rayon material.

Although I was only about six months pregnant, by the time we reached the camp meeting in Liberal, Kansas, I looked like I could have the baby any day. This concerned some of the people at the camp. We still had a few more meetings on the drive home, so some couples got together and decided to send the 4 wives home early— by train on a Pullman car. We hated to leave our husbands, but finally agreed to go—and it was pure luxury to sleep in a bed on the train.

Our type of travel was to push the car when it ran out of gas. We sometimes limped into a small town with car trouble. But the LORD was always with us. Near disasters turned into blessings. One car had tie rods that broke as we came into a town in the Rocky Mountains. If they had broken and we had lost our steering, we probably would have gone over the edge into a deep canyon.

In all the years of travel and thousands of miles covered, there was never a serious accident of any kind. GOD's timing was always perfect—and I'm sure we had an army of angels surrounding us. They were probably pretty beat up by the time their replacements came.

Another sideline...All of the guys had jobs or were going to school part time and were free in the summer months. That's why we could travel at this time. Dick taught school at Greenleaf Academy in Idaho for a few years. Although he had other classes, music was the main reason he went to Greenleaf. The school was very small and most of the kids were in his choir—and the choir was good!

Dick took his choir to the State Music Festival, and even though it was the smallest school, they took first place and were chosen to perform at the final concert. They were picked over the largest *school –Boise, the capital of Idaho. So Boise wanted Dick to come and teach music there. We still don't know how they managed to find us that summer, but about every week Dick would get a phone call from the Boise School District—offering him a job. Each time the offer got better and the salary higher. But as we prayed about it, we felt we were still committed to Greenleaf Academy—even though the pay from Boise was about three or four times more money.*

Back to the camp meeting in Kansas...When Dick felt he should give 10% extra to support a missionary, he consulted and prayed with me first. This was important, because we were barely making enough money to survive while teaching at Greenleaf. I agreed with him—although I had no idea how we could make it. But to this day, we have never had a bill we couldn't pay. We have never felt deprived or lacked anything. GOD will not be a debtor to any person.

Dick forgot to mention our time in Plainview, Kansas—a small town where the guys had meetings for several days. One woman who had a big farmhouse was gone for a few weeks, but had told the church we could all stay in her house together. We thought this was great—we enjoyed staying with other people, but once in a while we needed a break like this. And it was a good experience, but there was one problem—no indoor plumbing. The "out house" was "single," and there were 8 adults. We finally figured a way to tell when it was in use. We had flags, which we tied to the door—red meant "in use" and white was "all-clear."

Probably one of the most memorable experiences we had was when we crossed the bridge into Brooklyn. We had always heard about the Brooklyn accent and their street fights. But we thought it was just exaggerated for movies and television. However, the minute we crossed over into Brooklyn it was like entering another country— and they lived up to everything we had ever heard or seen in the movies. Within minutes we saw our first, of many, street fights. And then we heard them speak. But the time that impressed me most was when the woman went crazy in the cafeteria where we were eating. After she destroyed Dick's dinner, she came to the drinking glasses where I was watching in amazement. When she threw the glasses on the floor, shattered pieces of glass landed all over my legs and feet. We almost felt like we were part of a wild movie, but decided it must be reality. We really were the wide-eyed "country cousins" in the big city for the first time.

Now about the four wives singing at the Barbershop Contest in Oregon, we were not the ones that decided to enter—our husbands signed us up as contestants! I can't recall if we had eight or ten children at that time between us—but it was enough to keep us plenty busy. And we didn't live very close at that time. We certainly didn't expect to win anything, but it was a fun experience. We always said there were: 4 Flats, 4 Sharps, and eventually, 18 Naturals.

Since our children were so close in age, we all had boys about the same size. With a lot of coaching from their mothers, they did a surprise imitation of their fathers at a college program—singing the Four Flats introduction song and "Dry Bones"—complete with the actions and straw hats and canes. The quartet was hysterical, and the audience went wild. I think the boys were all pre-school—at least they were very young.

Paul Thornburg joins us while Chris is called to duty

The Four Sharps in old fashioned garb

Crescent Mailbox

Dear Miss Shattuck:

Since hearing the "Four Flats" in chapel this morning I have written a bit of verse expressing the thoughts which came to me. If you should like to print this in the Crescent you may.

THE WIVES

We all look up to the "Four Flats"
And think they are just fine,
But who has thought of their
   brave little wives—
The girls who are left behind?

The "Flats" are brilliant—they're
   witty.
More talent you cannot find;
But my "hat's off" to the brave
   little wives—
The girls who are left behind!

The boys are singing the Gospel,
They'll open the eyes of the blind
And souls will be saved forever;
But their wives are left behind.

Oh, pray for the boys—pray daily!
May God, by His Spirit, remind;
And, as you pray, remember
The wives who are left behind.

And when God writes the records
   in Heaven
I'm sure therein we'll find

That He gave a special notice
To the wives who stayed behind.

Sincerely,
Mrs. Elva Neifert.

Chapter 17

CALLING IT QUITS

It was 1960 and World Vision had changed quite dramatically from the old days when we first joined. Our children were beginning to feel the effects of fathers being gone from home so much. It was time to put our families first and find jobs that would allow us to be home more. Besides, World Vision had enough of our songs recorded for broadcast that they didn't need us in the studio each week.

The question would come up from time to time, "What should we do?" Driving down the highway one day Helen said, "What about the mission field? We've always said we were willing to go to the mission field." "Yes, but we're too old. No one would accept us. Besides, we have five kids," I retorted. "But we've never made ourselves available." Helen shot back.

That was it, we had to find out. So we babysat the kids and headed to the coast where we holed up in a motel and spent the next few days in prayer and reading the Bible. After about three days we came upon this scripture in Hebrews 13:5 (Amplified):

"Let your character or moral disposition be free from love of money – including greed, avarice, lust and craving for earthly possessions – and be satisfied with your present circumstances and with what you have; for He (God) Himself has said, I will not in any way fail you nor give you up nor leave you without support. I will not, I will not, I will not in any degree leave you helpless, nor forsake, nor let you down or relax My hold on you, assuredly not."

What more was there to be said? We knew without a shadow of a doubt that we had to make ourselves available. We were convinced no mission would have us and that would settle everything, but we were committed to one thing. We would be available.

Immediately, it came to my mind that we should apply to Overseas Crusades where the quartet had such a good ministry in the Philippines. I knew they needed teachers at Faith Academy in the Philippines and I had a background in teaching, so it might be possible.

When we arrived back home in Glendora, there on my desk were five letters offering me jobs in five different places. One was as Youth for Christ director in Hawaii. Another was as television director for Youth for Christ in Portland, another as youth director in a large church and on and on it went.

If I had received any one of these offers before we went to the beach, no doubt, I would have jumped at one of these chances, but God knew He wanted us to be alone where He could get our attention. It wasn't long before we heard back from Overseas Crusades with a "Yes, we need you."

Chris was busy deciding what he should do, too. In the end he took the job of youth director at Lake Avenue Congregational Church in Pasadena, California. He later went on to become Chaplain of the Brown Military Academy in Azusa, California. In 1967 he became Chaplain of George Fox College, our old alma mater, where he served for eighteen years and retired as chaplain emeritus.

After two years Harlow went back to Newberg to become the editor of the printing and publishing ministry of Barclay Press, the printing arm of the Friends Church of the Northwest. After about 15 years there Harlow moved to the Oregon coast where he became the director of Twin Rocks Friends Campground, another ministry of the Friends Church.

Norval decided to stay on with World Vision as assistant to Bob Pierce. Bob needed someone to be at his beck and call 24 hours a day and that is about what Norval was asked to do. Until Bob Pierce died a few years later, Norval was there by his side, helping in many personal ways as well as with business problems. Norval stayed on with World Vision for 28 more years. In 1972 he moved to Oregon and was the Superintendent of the Northwest Yearly Meeting of Friends for eight years. Norval then went back to World Vision until 1992 when he went to Denver to be Director of Evangelical Friends Mission. He is now chaplain at Quaker Gardens Retirement Center in California.

Helen's Comments…

By the time the quartet felt they should quit, we had 18 children between us. We all were convinced it was the right thing to do, but it wasn't easy. We had become so much a part of each other and our lives were so integrated with all of the others that it was like a family separating. The children probably felt it as much as anyone did. They were known as "The Quartet Kids"—and I think they felt it was an honor and maybe made them a little famous. But it was the loss of each other that hurt the most.

We all wanted to do the LORD's will, but Dick and I weren't sure what that was. I remember Norv saying to us, "GOD wants us to do His will even more than we want to do it. If we are really willing for anything, then we can rest assured that He won't let us make a mistake. He opens and closes doors and keeps us in His will." When you have five children to take care of, you sure don't want to make a mistake. Norval's advice really helped us.

It wasn't easy waiting to find out what we were going to do. After making ourselves available, we still had to wait for the mission's decision. Even though we knew they wouldn't take us, we knew we had to wait for their answer. And it was hard—waiting is always hard. We couldn't take any permanent job until we heard from O.C. But we still had to live—bills to pay, children to feed, etc. Dick and I both did substitute teaching and other jobs, but the LORD had other lessons to teach us too (besides patience and trusting Him!) One of them had to do with hospitality.

About the time when we were at our lowest financially, we had a guest, an "uninvited" guest—and I resented him. The quartet had met him during their travels, and he made our home his headquarters for several weeks. Even feeding our small children took real planning, but he was a big man and ate ravenously. He could be gone most of the day, but he managed to show up just as we sat down to eat. He never offered to pay for anything.

Over the years, Dick and I had become very anti-social. The quartet was gone so much of the time that when Dick was home we wanted to spend our time with each other and the children—we didn't want intruders.

Almost to the point of telling our "boarder" it was time for him to leave, we again read our special promise in Hebrews 13:5. But this time we studied the whole chapter. We got as far as the second verse and the LORD was right in the room talking to us again. Only this time He cautioned, "Do not forget or neglect or refuse to extend hospitality to strangers (in the brotherhood)—being friendly, cordial, and gracious, sharing the comforts of your home and doing your part generously—for through it some have entertained angels without knowing it."

All the time that I had been disliking this man, the children had been loving him—his jovial personality and constant jokes. Dick and I decided that if this man was from the LORD, we'd better change our attitude toward him. So with GOD's help we began acting differently. We laughed at his jokes—they really were funny. We welcomed him when he appeared at meal times, even when there wasn't enough food to go around. Before we realized what was happening, we actually began to enjoy him, and he even drew our family closer together.

As so often happens, when our attitude is transformed, circumstances also change. I opened the refrigerator door one day and found it full of food, special things we had not had for weeks. A few days later a note of thanks appeared on the kitchen table. Tucked inside was money. We really needed that lesson. When we went to the Philippines we had guests constantly. For almost five years we averaged about 50 guest meals a month. We met incredible people and both Dick and I and our children loved having company. We spent 32 wonderful years in the Philippines

ROSE HOWERTER/The Oregonian

Back for more: The winners of the first two Barber Shop Ballad contests 50 years ago sing again Saturday in Forest Grove. They are (from left) Dick Cadd, Ron Crecelius, Norval Hadley and Harlow Ankeny.

Four Flats return to triumph site

■ Members of the senior quartet find that wind and range have faded through the years, but their impact remains

By PETER SLEETH
of The Oregonian staff

FOREST GROVE — The Four Flats trundled up the backstage steps Saturday night, maybe a little wiser, definitely a lot older and with all the kinks of age.

The quartet quickly crooned its way through a medley of barbershop ballads, bowed to an approving crowd, then dropped backstage again.

"I didn't have any wind," complained Harlow Ankeny, 67, after the performance.

"I didn't have any range," said Ron Crecelius, 75.

But they had the crowd.

The Four Flats and dozens of other performers made the 50th annual Original All Northwest Barbershop Ballad Contest a success.

It ended Saturday evening. About 18 quartets competed for cash prizes in performances peppered with cancan dancers and a women's chorus.

Nearly 3,000 people attended the two-day event, said Don Paulson, one of the organizers.

The contest winners follow:

■ First place — Harmonic Tremors, from Bremerton and Lynden, Wash.

■ Second — Extra Extra, from Seattle, Portland and Olympia.

■ Third — Audio Synchrasy, from Newberg, Portland and Milwaukie.

■ Fourth — Dice, from Portland and Salem.

■ Fifth — Fascination, from Seattle area.

■ Sixth — The Aliens, from Portland area.

■ Seventh — The Peanut Butter Conspiracy, from Klamath Falls, Medford, Salem and Beaverton.

■ Eighth — Chord Jesters, from Cottage Grove, Elmira, Eagle Point and Klamath Falls.

First place brings an award of $500 in silver dollars; second, $350 in silver dollars; and third, $300 in silver dollars.

In 1947, the Four Flats wowed the crowd for the first time at the first Barbershop Ballad Contest held in this Tualatin Valley town. Their first-place win then launched them on a singing career that took them around the world until they broke up in 1962.

"We sang overseas for everything from lepers to presidents," Crecelius said.

The Four Flats went their separate ways after 1962, landing in different states and different jobs. But today, all but one of the members has returned to Newberg to live, and, when the audience calls, to sing.

"It changed our whole lives," Crecelius said of that one night in 1947.

"We feel blessed," Ankeny said.

EPILOGUE

We don't know if we are the longest living quartet to ever survive or not. One thing we do know; we probably have had more "farewell" concerts than any other quartet.

Even though I was in the Philippines for 32 years, I usually got home every few years and each time, there would be one more "farewell" concert! There were times when I was in the States for something other than furlough and we would be asked to sing "one more time."

On one occasion, the town people of Newberg planned a large concert to be held in the largest auditorium available. It was the high school gymnasium and they even had backup singers to accompany us. We decided that time was catching up to us, so we practiced and learned some of the modern songs of the day, such as "What the World Needs Now is Love Sweet Love" and a few others.

The concert was to be recorded – live. That doesn't sound so bad on the surface, but when you realize that we hadn't sung together for a few years and had very little time for rehearsal and we were singing some new songs, it gave us a case of nerves. The recording came off so good though, that it was one of our greatest selling records. It had to be made into a double LP because of the length of the concert.

The concert was the middle of February and it started snowing that afternoon. We thought no one would show up. To our amazement, the gym was packed with people who came from several states around. That night we were to sing in Salem, Oregon, and we slipped and slid all the way there. We could hardly believe that so many would come out on a snowy afternoon to our concert. They said it was the largest crowd ever to gather in Newberg.

During our years with World Vision we made three long-play records. Dick Anthony was the producer of "Jesus is Calling." He used Capitol Records studio in Hollywood and engaged several professional musicians to accompany us. I remember we used Jack Benny's drummer and other well-known musicians. Dick used mostly songs from our own repertoire, but also included others and some of his own compositions.

The other two records were made especially for World Vision at Word Records and included lots of missionary numbers and songs we had used on the World Vision broadcast. Dick Bolks was our producer then.

When the 50th year anniversary of the Forest Grove Barbershop Contest rolled around we were invited to appear as special guests. Though we were not as good as when we first won the Championship 50 years earlier, the audience were very appreciative of four old men who made a valiant effort.

On the occasion of the Centennial Celebration of George Fox College, we were called on to open the celebration, and since I was still home on furlough, we were asked to close the year with one more concert. It was a great tribute to us, as a quartet, and a reminder that we had come a long way with a very understanding alma mater and very good roots under us.

Helen's Comments...

People couldn't seem to let the quartet quit—which was fine with me. I never got tired of hearing them, and I wanted our children to remember them forever. We still felt like "The Four-Flats Family." Many people (including family) always looked forward to every concert with great anticipation.

Their recordings were excellent. My favorite was "JESUS is Calling"—and although they never thought anything was quite good enough—when they listened to it years later they realized it was exceptional. When we were in the Philippines, we heard it being played over the radio constantly. When we came home on furlough we heard it again as we were driving down the highway. So I guess other people liked it too. We heard the story of a man who came to know JESUS because of the record. But he never heard the record! He was walking through a record store one day and saw the title..."JESUS is Calling." The LORD spoke to him through the title and called him to JESUS. It's very interesting how GOD works to draw people to Himself.

When the guys made the records, a problem surfaced. Most of them couldn't read music very much. They usually just practiced their songs in the car while they were traveling. If they had heard it, they could usually sing it—with all of their parts. They didn't need written notes—the chords they "heard" were usually far superior. But Dick Anthony wrote some special arrangements for them, and sent them home to learn their parts. So we stayed up half the night while I went over each part on the piano with them. They learned fast.

There are so many things that my husband forgot to mention, and when all the guys and their wives get together we could go on for hours. We all seem to remember different stories too. Besides singing for Presidents of countries, Dick forgot to tell about singing on the same program with Dale Evans and Pat Boone and Ronald Reagan (and others I can't remember). Dick was sitting next to Ronald Reagan when people began coming behind them and asking for Ronald's autograph. Dick had to put his packet of music on Reagan's knee to give support for the signature. Dick likes to tell people he helped Ronald Reagan sign autographs.

I will admit it's a little different kind of life when your husband can't get dressed until he finds out what three other guys are wearing. But because of the quartet and their influence and popularity (not only in the U.S., but in other countries as well), here are some of the benefits:

- *Our financial and prayer support as missionaries came much easier*
- *Our work in Manila had a head start—Dick was already "famous"*
- *We were privileged to attend Presidential Prayer Breakfasts—both U.S. and Manila*
- *The Billy Graham team came to our home for lunch in the Philippines*
- *We were able to be on television and also produce TV shows*
- *We had an unbelievable "millionaire type" vacation with Norv & Mary in Hawaii—almost free—because someone knew the quartet*
- *Because of a mutual quartet friend, we got invited to a private dinner with the American Ambassador—at their home in Manila*
- *We have friends all over the world*

- *Our quartet "family" has a special bond that most people never know*

I'm sure there are many more benefits that I will think of later, but we have been blessed beyond words. "Now glory be to GOD who by His mighty power at work within us is able to do far more than we could ever dare to ask or even dream of—infinitely beyond our highest prayers, desires, thoughts, or hopes. May He be given glory forever and ever through endless ages because of his master plan of salvation for the church through JESUS CHRIST." Eph. 3:20 THANK YOU LORD!

Update at the time of this writing, 2003:

Chris is 82 years old and has 11 grandchildren; 7 great grandchildren
Dick is 79 years old and has 13 grandchildren; 4 great grandchildren
Norval is 75 years old and has 6 grandchildren
Harlow is 74 years old and has 13 grandchildren

POST SCRIPT

On June 12, 2003 Norval and Mary Hadley took a vacation from their work at Quaker Gardens near Garden Grove, California, and came to Newberg for just one day. The three of us in the quartet who live in Newberg arranged for a breakfast at the local Shari's restaurant, because the Hadleys had to leave shortly after breakfast.

It was a great reunion getting Norval and Mary caught up with all the local news. Helen asked our daughter, Yvonne, to come and take a few pictures of this rare event. Of course, we talked about our latest aches and pains and reminded ourselves that we were now senior citizens and had slipped into the category of all people advancing in age. We caught up on the latest news of our kids and grandkids. There was some reminiscing and of course, we had to see if we could still sing. Norval suggested the spiritual, <u>Behold the Bridegroom Cometh</u>. With a little stretching for words we sang it straight through. Our wives were ecstatic. They raved and raved about how good we still were. We knew they wanted to encourage us.

We stayed in this private dining room for two and a half hours. Outside in the restaurant no one knew that history was being made in the private room in the back. Perhaps this was the last time these four men would be together as a quartet until one day when they will each join that heavenly choir.